Christopher Radko's

Heart of Christmas

Christopher Radko's
Heart of Christmas

Text by Olivia Bell Buehl
Photographs by Keith Scott Morton

CLARKSON POTTER/PUBLISHERS
NEW YORK

Copyright © 2001 by Christopher Radko
Photographs copyright © 2001 by Keith Scott Morton

Published by Clarkson Potter/Publishers,
New York, New York.
Member of the Crown Publishing Group.
Random House, Inc. New York, Toronto, London, Sydney, Auckland
www.randomhouse.com
CLARKSON N. POTTER is a trademark
and POTTER and colophon are registered
trademarks of Random House, Inc.
Printed in Japan

Design by Jennifer Napier and Grace Lee

Library of Congress Cataloging-in-Publication Data
Radko, Christopher.
Christopher Radko's Heart of Christmas / by Christopher Radko;
text by Olivia Bell Buehl.—[2nd ed.].
p. cm.
1. Radko, Christopher.   2. Christmas decorations.
I. Buehl, Olivia Bell.   II. Title.
TT900.C4 R34   2001
745.594'12—dc21   00-069870

ISBN 0-609-60475-9
10 9 8 7 6 5 4 3 2 1
First Edition

Contents

Acknowledgments

This book represents the goodness and good work of many, many people. First, let me extend my appreciation to members of my staff who generously gave of their time, despite their already heavy workloads: Kyle Hall, Janet Bucknor, Nancy Kunz, and Timothy Scalet. I must single out Timothy for special thanks. As leader of my visual merchandising team, he coordinated the efforts of an extraordinary crew: Jorge Betancourt, David Monzione, Edward McCay, Todd Moss, Patrick Gregware, Jo Ann Williams, Steve Hardwick, Jane Gavigan, Richard Baugher, Pamela Hardesty, and Linda Kane. Their efforts were invaluable in creating the magic that talented photographer Keith Scott Morton has captured in his evocative photographs. Thanks also to photo stylist Kim Freeman and to Keith's associates: Tara Striano, Debra DeBoise, Eric Richards, Robert Bucham, Rob Hadlow, and Barry Johnson; and to Kim's assistant, Maureen Clark.

Many thanks to my editor, Margot Schupf, who first envisioned *Heart of Christmas* and gracefully steered its passage through the complicated course of illustrated book publishing. My gratitude also to Lauren Shakely, Marysarah Quinn, Caitlin Israel, and Mark McCauslin at Clarkson Potter. And kudos to Jennifer Napier for her superb design.

I sincerely appreciate all the homeowners who graciously opened their doors to our crew: Jocelyn and Chris Hayes, David Frieman, Wanda and Greg Furman, Radko staffers Tom Branthaver and Randall Viestenz, Duncan and Debbie Brown, Van and Iris Christo, Glenn and Ann Sather, and Dusty Phair. Sheryl and Marc Green welcomed us into their home and let us raid their store, Lux Bond & Green, for beautiful china, glassware, and other domestic treasures. Lindsey Whitaker and Judy Howe also pitched in.

Christmas memorabilia collector Fred Cannon gave us the keys to his marvelous Brooklyn row house; he also proved an invaluable resource for information on antique ornaments. Thanks also to Julia Weede, Suzanne Pandich, David Ware, Laura Turansick, Monica Cabral, and Stephania Brown of the Lyndhurst staff; and to Governor John Rowland and First Lady Patricia Rowland of Connecticut, and to Jo McKenzie, Darren Cugno, and the rest of residence staff.

As a gardener myself, I stand in awe of the magnificent efforts of florists Marlo Phillips of Marlo Flowers; Melissa Sorman; Elissa Rinaldo of Petals & Stems; J. Wright Flowers; and Bruce Roblin, Pat Scrivener, Paul Jarvas, and Joanne Tennant of White's Flowers. Heartfelt thanks to our Canadian crew: Warner E. Einer, Nevin Merrells, Max Radford, Avalene Adshead, Dianne Einer, Maurice Routley, T. J. Bews, Rob Hadlow, Bill Merrett, Tom Edwards, John Jones, Craig Lazdins, Jonas Owens, Brent Osborne, Tim Milligan, John Dambrauskas, and Kim Funk. My favorite Christmas tree grower, Eric Sundback, shared his wisdom-and a few of his magnificent trees. Christopher Krupa of The Curio Cabinet and Christmas Village of Olde Worthington was equally helpful in explaining the intricacies of artificial Christmas trees.

Finally, thanks to my collaborator, Olivia Bell Buehl, without whom this book simply would not be. She not only wrote the lively text but found the locations, organized the shoots, and brought all our work together. Bravo, Olivia!

Introduction

Symbols and rituals make up the fabric of our lives. At their most basic, these rituals derive from the seasonal calendar, enabling man to feel connected to the natural world. They also help us understand who we are in the context of family, community, and the human race. Every culture has its defining festivals, and without doubt, Christmas is our country's predominant holiday. But it's important to realize that this wonderful season represents not just a Christian holiday. The celebration we now call Christmas hearkens back to the late-fall and midwinter festivals of the ancient world that celebrated the bounty of the harvest and offered hope that fertility would return in the spring. Our feelings about Christmas are so passionate because they are primal. Moreover, Christ's message of hope, love, and the essential goodness of the human spirit transcends a single faith. In our culture, Christmas serves as receptacle for these traditions and emotions, but Kwanza, Hanukkah, and the winter solstice are equally meaningful.

PREVIOUS PAGE: **A fresh snowfall, a lighted tree, and a few metal snowflake ornaments create a magical effect at dusk.** ABOVE: **A rustic birdhouse signals the season with a pine garland and a tiny pepperberry wreath.** OPPOSITE: **A Santa made by Canadian artisan Kathy Patterson sports a lambswool beard and holds a feather tree and a bundle of toys.**

The traditions of Christmas also offer an antidote to our breakneck-pace and often throwaway society, providing a place where we can feel centered and secure. We live in an era where the only constant is change, where our computers and cell phones are obsolete long before they wear out, and where age is considered a liability instead of grounds for respect. Celebrating year after year the holiday that evolved from those ancient festivals also helps us to connect past and present in an unbroken chain that links us to our forebears. In this way, holidays allow us to transcend time, participate in family traditions, and feel part of a continuous piece of human history. Christmas gives us an opportunity to reflect upon and celebrate what is enduring, even eternal.

Long before the birth of Christ, our ancestors responded to the natural cycles of the calendar with festivals and rituals that gave a human dimension to forces greater than them-

selves. When the days shortened and turned cold, our forebears naturally looked to the spirit world for answers. Many pagan rituals, such as bringing a Yule log into the house, hanging sprigs of mistletoe, and lighting candles at the window, were eventually absorbed into the Christian holiday. Although they may no longer be imbued with their original meaning, these customs still resonate within our hearts. To ancient peoples, evergreen plants signified that warmth, light, and fertility would indeed rebound. By bringing green boughs into their homes, they honored the spirits that they believed controlled the seasons. Today we may not believe in wood sprites, but decorating with boughs of holly has become an integral part of holiday celebrations, raising our midwinter spirits.

When we celebrate Christmas, we honor our ancestors, even if we have never met them, keeping their memory alive in traditions handed down from one generation to another. Continuing family customs is very important to me. In 1983, our family tree adorned with more than a thousand cherished ornaments crashed to the ground. Those glass treasures had been collected over decades by four generations of my family, and their destruction also meant the loss of a repository of family memories. My Polish grandmother was particularly

Power in numbers: A quintet of plastic snowmen made in the 1950s and '60s glow from within. Electrical cords hide behind the stone ledge.

devastated. In my desire to replace the ornaments, make amends to my grandmother, and restore the way our family traditionally celebrated Christmas, I traveled to Poland to find glassblowers who could replicate the vintage mouth-blown ornaments. That is how my ornament business began.

Perhaps the best part of Christmas is the anticipation. Who doesn't recall lying in bed as a child, wondering what Santa would bring when day finally dawned? As an adult, anticipation extends to excitement about the arrival of relatives, to wondering if our kids will be pleased with their gifts, if we will find the perfect Christmas tree, and if snow might actually fall this year. For me, the sense of expectation includes a feeling that anything is possible. Christmas gives us permission to be childlike again, no matter what our age.

Christmas restores our sense of wonder

and joyousness, the part of us that is closest to God. The scent of pine or balsam immediately transports me to my childhood lying under the Christmas tree, imagining that all the twinkling lights were the countless millions of stars that fill the nighttime sky.

By entering into holiday preparations in a spirit of celebration rather than of duty, you can avoid the burnout that often accompanies the season. In a very real way, those of us who love the rituals surrounding Christmas are preparing something sacred, and the temple for this ceremony is the home. Decorating for the holidays is not just about appearance; it is a doorway to deeper meaning. When fresh greenery and cherished decorations are hung with joy, purpose, and a sense of continuity with the past, they transcend simple

Vintage Shiny-Brite glass ornaments, known for their pastel coloring, were originally made in the United States in the 1940s and '50s. Hot items on eBay, the ornaments enjoy enhanced value when in their original boxes. My company, Christopher Radko, has recently revived the line.

décor and feed the soul. They make our homes into places that nurture our own hearts and souls and those of the people we love. Christmas decorations also create a magical environment that speaks to the child in us.

Likewise, if entertaining friends and family at Christmastime were just about assuaging their physical hunger any meal would suffice. But we are responding to a desire to nurture them on another level: to delight them with delicacies, yes, but also to offer what their spirit longs for, in the form of a traditional feast. In our fast-paced culture, our souls often go hungry. Filling our homes with the true spirit of Christmas nurtures the part of us that food or material possessions can't satisfy.

Christmas offers an open channel to our hearts. The portal may be an ornament passed down by your great-grandmother, a recipe for wassail in your grandmother's flowery script, candy-striped stockings knitted by your mother, a carol your father loved to sing at the piano, or a crèche built by your grandfather. Each generation adds its own flourishes to traditions so that when all the strands are woven together, the fabric becomes still longer and stronger. And, like everything in this great country, traditions from many cultures have become part of our melting pot. Whether straw ornaments from Scandinavia, a French cake called *bûche de Noël,* or the delicate Polish art of paper cutouts, the United States has welcomed and absorbed them all.

I love to celebrate this wonderfully inclusive holiday with plentitude, passion, color, and exuberance. Christmas infuses all our senses in a way that confirms the beauty of our physical lives. We exist simultaneously on the physical and the spiritual plane. The scents of savory food, the sound of music, the visual stimulus of beauty can all be paths to the spiritual realm. Nature is also a portal to the spiritual world.

ABOVE: **A topiary made of tiny glass ornaments finds a compatible home in front of a 19th-century leaded-glass roundel. Boughs of greenery, French wired ribbons, and Radko glass globes, garlands, and beaded stars complete the ornate arrangement.**
OPPOSITE: **A brick town house in Brooklyn dons classic Christmas finery: garlands of greens wrapped with hundreds of miniature amber lights, eight beribboned wreaths, and a candle in every window.**

In addition to the gifts and food and other sensual pleasures that attract us, we are also drawn to the holiday because it symbolizes humanity's highest ideals. Visualize world peace. Be a good neighbor, and a good partner to your spouse or lover; donate your time to a worthy cause, and open your pocketbook—and your heart—to those less fortunate than you. The true spirit of the season reminds us to rise above our baser instincts and transform ourselves into the people we know we can be. You can instill in your self-limiting adulthood the childhood belief in infinite possibilities.

So turn off your mind for a few minutes and think with your heart. Our minds tell us that Santa doesn't fly through the sky and squeeze down every chimney in the land, but in our hearts we know his *energy* is real, that the *spirit* of giving that he encompasses is real. His energy is represented in an open heart, in jollity, and in a giving nature. Everything he represents exists in all of us; Santa challenges us to put that goodness back in ourselves, rather like a good spiritual workout. Our society buys into that idea once a year. You won't want to keep your tree up 365 days a year, but I propose we live that spirit year-round, rather than using Christmas to make up for everything we have done the rest of the year. Just as our ancient forebears came together at winter festivals, let us come together as a community in the face of the unknown and unknowable and rejoice anyway!

Christopher Radko

THE WELL-DRESSED CHRISTMAS TREE

WITH ALL DUE RESPECT TO SANTA, THE CENTRAL ICON
OF THE SEASON IS THE CHRISTMAS TREE. I CAN'T
IMAGINE THE HOLIDAYS WITHOUT THE MAGIC OF
WONDERFULLY DECORATED TREES, EACH DIFFERENT,
EACH SPECIAL. LIKE THE HEARTH OR A DINING TABLE,
A CHRISTMAS TREE DRAWS PEOPLE TO IT—AND TO ONE
ANOTHER. OUR VISCERAL RESPONSE TO EVERGREENS
MAKES ME WONDER IF THEY HAVE MAGICAL PROPERTIES
WE HAVE LONG FORGOTTEN. THE SCENTS OF PINE,
SPRUCE, AND FIR TREES NOT ONLY CONNECT US TO
THE NATURAL WORLD, THEY ACTUALLY CHEER AND
INVIGORATE US. NO WONDER AROMATHERAPISTS USE
THE ESSENTIAL OILS OF EVERGREENS FOR THEIR
ENERGIZING AND HEALING PROPERTIES.

A Christmas tree serves as a diary of a family's history: Each ornament records a moment in the lives of its members. As you unwrap your ornaments you might recall that your angel tree topper was a gift from a dear friend. The little glass birds from the Paris flea market remind you of a vacation a decade ago. You think of your favorite great-aunt when you open the vintage glass icicles she gave you, still in their original cardboard box. And so it goes, with trinkets marking the births of children and their own clumsily crafted ornaments made of dough and paper recording the passage of years. All these fragments of your life hang on the tree and shine back at you, reminding you of who you are as well as the meaning of the holiday. That's why I think of a Christmas tree as having the same evocative qualities as a photo album or a personal art gallery.

Immigrant Influences

Ubiquitous as it is today, the idea of bringing a fresh-cut tree inside and covering it with trinkets was not in general practice in this country until the middle of the nineteenth century. The practice of decorating a Christmas tree originated in Germany (see "Ancient Origins" on page 27), and it was Germany that played a major role in shaping our Christmas customs. We don't know definitively where and when the first decorated Christmas trees appeared in our country; we do know that the charming custom of the *Tannenbaum* came to our shores with people of German birth. Pennsylvania German settlers are said to have decorated community trees as early as 1747, and the custom of the family tree may have originated with the Moravians of Bethlehem, Pennsylvania, in the very early 1800s. Others claim that Hessian soldiers stationed at Trenton, New Jersey, in 1776 were the first in this country to cut down firs and decorate them.

But not all colonial Americans celebrated Christmas. The Puritans of Massachusetts banned its observance. Many Northerners continued to consider

PREVIOUS PAGE: **Fabric ornaments by Gladys Boalt depicting children's book characters adorn a tree in Fred Cannon's home.** ABOVE: **A feather tree, set in an angel papier-mâché tree stand, is hung with antique angels, made of glass, bisque, and wax.** OPPOSITE: **A tree in the study at the governor of Connecticut's mansion welcomes visitors.**

For old-fashioned country appeal, this fir tree wears chains made from loops of red and green grosgrain ribbon, an update on the construction-paper versions made by schoolchildren. Snowflakes cut from foil paper and stars crafted from stalks of wheat and red embroidery floss lend other homemade touches. Supplying glitter and glow are hundreds of 19th-century-style Radko ornaments and old-fashioned C-7 lightbulbs. The "Twilight Santa" finial has two indents, or reflectors, that play with light. Radko glass garlands are hung vertically instead of in the usual swagged treatment.

Christmas celebrations as rowdy and sinful, instead regarding
Thanksgiving as the true American holiday. On the other hand,
Southerners participated in all-out Christmas celebrations as a key
part of the social season. It is not surprising that the first state to
make Christmas a legal holiday was Alabama in 1836, followed by
Louisiana and Arkansas in 1938. The first decorated Christmas tree
in the White House appeared in 1856 during the administration of
President Franklin Pierce. After the Civil War, the celebration of
Christmas was finally well established throughout the country.

Jewelry for the Tree

Commercially made ornaments of silver and gilt foil and cardboard
began appearing in the United States in the 1870s. By the 1880s,

printed figures embossed on paper became popular along with the new invention of spun-glass angel hair. But it was the invention of glass ornaments that was to transform the look of Christmas trees around the world. The town of Lauscha in the Thuringian Forest east of Nuremberg, Germany, had long been known for its glassblowers, skilled craftsmen who produced tiny glass beads for jewelry and dressmaking.

Early in the nineteenth century, the glassblowers found they could blow large glass bubbles, which they made when taking a break from their duties. They silvered the insides and lacquered the outsides of these big globes in bright colors just as they did their beads, and called them *Kugels*, German for "ball." Later, *Kugels* were blown into a mold to create a shape, such as an apple, a pear, an artichoke, or a cluster of grapes. Much too heavy to hang on a Christmas tree, *Kugels* were suspended from the ceiling, a candelabra, or a wooden frame. In addition

FAR LEFT: **An 1890s German revolving tree stand plays Christmas carols. The goose feather tree displays flat "Dresden" ornaments. Made of embossed die-cut cardboard to mimic gold or silver, they were made in 19th-century Germany.** ABOVE RIGHT: **Radko Little Gems, including "Snow White," "Petite Pierre," and "Gingerbread Chapel," some topped with bows, are perfectly sized for a tabletop tree. The "Royal Shine" finial, a scaled-down version of a Radko classic, and 4-inch icicles are in perfect proportion.**

to their beauty, they were useful in adding reflected illumination to dim, candlelit rooms.

In 1867, a gasworks built in Lauscha pioneered technology that allowed a flame to remain at a consistently high temperature, making it possible to create large, thin-walled globes. The first true glass ornaments—light enough to hang on a tree branch—followed quickly. By 1870, Lauschan glass pinecones, acorns, Santas, fruits and vegetables, and birds were being exported to other European countries.

These delightful trinkets quickly became Victorian status symbols, dovetailing with the collection craze for which the era is famous. The popularity of the ornaments encouraged craftsmen to become more and more inventive. More than five thousand mold designs ensured a constant supply of ingenious subjects. Different but equally wonderful glass ornaments soon were being made in Poland and Bohemia (which later became Czechoslovakia, and later still, the Czech Republic). The glittering and playful decorations perfectly symbolized the joy and light of Christmas. By 1880 glass ornaments were being imported for sale in East Coast department stores. In 1890, F. W. Woolworth began selling them in his chain of five-and-ten-cent stores nationwide. Just before the outbreak of World War II, 95 percent of the glass ornaments sold in the United States had been crafted in and around Lauscha.

After decades in which machine-made ornaments were the norm, mouth-blown glass ornaments are enjoying a revival. I am proud to have played a major role in reinvigorating this craft.

Buying the Tree

But even the most beautiful ornaments cannot do the job alone. Selecting the right tree is crucial to getting the look you want. First, you need to decide on a real or an artificial tree or even a living tree with its roots balled in burlap. Each approach has its advantages and disadvantages. There are also many species of real trees to choose from (see "The Naked Truth" on page 186) and different types of manufactured trees (see "The Art of Artifice" on page 190).

If you have decided to go natural, you have the option of buying a cut tree or

OPPOSITE: **Fred Cannon's 11-foot-tall living room tree is laden with more than 2,000 lights and about as many German glass ornaments dating from 1870 to 1950. The early-19th-century Moravian star chandelier topping the tree is hung from the ceiling. A feather tree behind the wing chair holds more German glass ornaments and real wax candles (for looks only—they are never lighted).**
ABOVE: **The Yellow Kid, the very first comic strip character, is a rare find. Beside it a tin horseback rider sits on a glass ball wrapped in thinly spun tinsel. Below it a clip-on candleholder with a shade now glows from an electric bulb.**

going to a tree farm to cut down a live one. The former usually allows you more options in tree species; the latter offers a fresher tree. A cut tree you purchase in a church parking lot may have been harvested over a month earlier. Properly treated, a fresh-cut tree should last for up to eight weeks, according to West Virginia Christmas-tree grower Eric Sundback. Each tree farm tends to specialize in certain species. If you are set on a certain species, call ahead to make sure the farm grows what you are looking for. Many growers have found they can successfully raise trees not native to the area if climate and soil conditions are appropriate. If you do plan to buy at a tree lot, go early in the season when selection is best and the trees have not had time to dry out.

Another option is having a tree shipped directly to you from a tree farm. Although this approach may be more expensive (once you factor in shipping charges), you should be able to get exactly what you want in terms of species and size. (UPS handles trees up to seven feet tall.) And since the tree is not cut until you order it, it is likely to be fresher than trees from the neighborhood lot.

The Web is full of listings of growers around the country: Just direct your search engine to "Christmas" + "trees." To narrow your search, add the name of

Uncle Sam's Santa costume was sewn from an old flag and studded with vintage campaign buttons. An elephant and donkey jockey for attention at his feet. The flag umbrella belonged to an antique doll. A broken child's drum serves as a tree stand for the feather tree. The patriotic glass ornaments were made in Germany for the American market.

your state. The Web site grandly titled "All Christmas Tree Farms in the USA" (*www.christmas-tree.org/real/index*) actually delivers on its promise. Simply log in your state to find a list of growers in your area, as well as information on tree species, prices, and directions. There are also links to individual tree farms' Web sites. Nova Scotia–based PLC Resources (902-863-8000; *www.plc.ns.sympatico.ca*) will send you a balsam fir in a variety of sheared styles and a broad array of sizes. Mountain Star Farms (888-567-2981; *www.mtnstarfarms.com*) offers both Fraser and balsam firs. Blue Mountain Tree Farm (888-220-TREE; *www.freshchristmastrees.com*) delivers to your door a Douglas, Fraser, or Concolor fir ranging from five to seven feet tall.

Before you hop into the car (or go online), measure the height of the room where you plan to place the tree. The tree should be at least a foot shorter than the ceiling in the room where it will be set up, but don't leave so much space that

Small trees offer much more flexibility in placement than their larger relatives. TOP LEFT: Set in front of a robust antique French mirror, a stylized wire tree holds miniature Radko ornaments, among them "Just Desserts," "Midnight Blessings," and "Pretty Paper" gems. A swirl of silvery ribbon repeats the delicate curves of wire. A gauzy golden fabric draped loosely over the table softens the tableau, as does a sprinkling of faux rose petals. ABOVE: Highlighted against a red glazed wall, spun and molded cotton ornaments made in Germany in the 1920s and '30s cover a feather tree set on a butler's tray. At the base of the tree, a herd of cotton sheep gathers. Topping the tree is a cotton batting Santa dressed in a costume made of crepe paper. LEFT: Thousands of tiny glass beads strung on wire form this diminutive tree—it stands no more than a foot tall. The tiny lights are electrified. It was made as a gift; the recipient's first name is spelled out in the tiny blocks at the tree's base. Other items, including the tabby cat, also have personal relevance.

ABOVE: In the family room of the governor of Connecticut's mansion, a classic Radko tree takes pride of place. Hundreds of ornaments cluster so tightly that only the pyramidal form of the tree remains. Radko "Capulet Ball" tied with French wire ribbon bows, anchor the swagged greenery treatments over the windows. A coordinated spike tops the tree. Coppery icicles also dress up the greens. Another harlequin-pattern ornament hangs from the light fixture. Below, a Radko signature ornament, "The Great Tree," sits beside a wrapped gift. The model on the coffee table depicts the Georgian-style mansion. RIGHT: Conifers are not the only trees suitable for decoration. Two flowering orange trees in terra-cotta pots finished with velvety clump moss get holiday treatment with white-frosted star-shaped cookies.

it looks out of scale. (Take the height of your tree topper into consideration as well.) If the tree will be visible from all sides, make sure you find one that is uniformly well shaped. On the other hand, if the tree will be placed against a wall, you can probably get away with a few imperfections.

Choose a tree with a healthy green appearance, a strong aroma, and a minimum of brown needles. Needles should be flexible and remain firmly attached when you run a branch through your hand. To test for freshness, raise the tree a few inches off the ground, shake it, then drop it firmly on the butt end to see if needles adhere. Don't worry if a few inner brown needles drop off. Check the cut base for drops of sticky resin, indicating it was freshly cut. Also make sure the trunk of the tree is straight, particularly the bottom six to eight inches.

Setting Up the Tree

The right tree stand is absolutely essential to protect your tree and your precious ornaments. I had a disastrous experience eighteen years ago when I foolishly replaced our family tree stand with a shiny new one that turned out to be incapable of holding the twelve-foot tree. There are various types and styles of tree stands. Go for the best quality you can find (preferably heavy-gauge metal) and make sure the stand fits the diameter of the trunk. If the stand is too big, it may not hold the tree securely; too small and it simply can't contain the trunk. Some types allow you to compensate for an irregular trunk. Never shave down the sides of the trunk to fit a too-small stand. Not only will it be unstable, it could cause the tree to dry out prematurely. (For information on other containers, see "Underneath It All" on page 38.)

After strength, the most important characteristic of a stand is water capacity. According to the National

---

ANCIENT ORIGINS

The Christmas tree evolved from a blending of ancient customs. The early pagan Germans worshiped trees, which they regarded as symbols of life, hope, and fruitfulness, as well as home to tree sprites that provided protection against evil forces. According to legend, St. Boniface, the monk who organized the Christian church in England, came upon a group of pagan worshipers around a large oak tree, who were about to sacrifice a child to the god Thor. Boniface flattened the oak with one blow of his hand, and in its place a small fir tree sprang up. He told the pagans that the fir was the tree of life and represented the eternal life of Christ. Moreover, the fir's triangular shape was said to represent the Holy Trinity. The converted people turned their reverence from the oak to the fir tree. By the twelfth century in central Europe, fir trees were often hung upside down from ceilings at Christmastime.

Another ancient custom was to bring a tree branch into the house, where the fire's warmth would "force" it to produce blossoms early, presaging the arrival of spring. Christians adopted this custom, hoping the branch would bloom on Christmas Eve, symbolizing the redemption Christ offered to mankind. Beginning sometime around the eleventh century, priests employed miracle, or mystery, plays to teach the Christian religion since most common people could not read. To represent the tree in the Garden of Eden, apples and later Communion wafers (representing the Eucharist) were tied to the branches of fir trees. These were called trees of life, or paradise trees (*Paradiesbäume*). Finally, in the late Middle Ages a wooden pyramidal form, or *Lichtstock*, decorated with baubles, candles, and sprays of greenery appeared in Germany.

By the late sixteenth century these four customs had come together in Europe as the Christmas tree. The first detailed description of a decorated fir tree dates to 1601 in Strasbourg, Germany. Pastries were cut in the shapes of stars, angels, hearts, flowers, and bells; later cookies with a more secular theme depicted men, roosters, and other animals. Fruits and other food items symbolized plenty; red flowers represented knowledge; white, innocence. In time, gingerbread, wax, and marzipan became raw materials for delightful figures.

Christmas Tree Association, a good rule of thumb is one quart of water daily for every inch of the tree trunk's diameter. So, a tree with a four-inch diameter, which is average for a six-foot tree, would require a tree stand with a capacity of one gallon of water, but this is the bare minimum; you would have to refill it daily. Once a tree dries out, it cannot be refreshed. If you have a vintage decorative tree stand, be sure that it is still in working order and use it only for trees of appropriate size and dimension. Since it may not have an adequate container for water, you may prefer to use it for a feather tree.

Take a minute to put some of your favorite Christmas music on the CD player to get in the mood. Then, before you even think about decorating, step back and regard your tree. Is it perfectly straight? Is the best side facing you when you enter the room? Is it too bushy at the bottom where you want to set up a tableau? Or does it seem sparse in one area? This is the time to remedy any natural fail-

ings. To remedy bushiness at the base, simply remove a few bottom branches, standing back to survey your work after each amputation. If foliage around the base seems scrawny and you have height to spare, simply retrim the trunk and set the tree up again. If there are empty areas elsewhere on the tree, tie or wire adjacent branches together to enhance fullness.

Lighting the Way

To get the blazing glow that is a trademark of a Radko tree, I recommend wrapping lights. Compared to stringing lights over the branches, wrapping is deliberate and far more labor intensive. On an 8-foot artificial tree, we may use as many as 3,000 bulbs. A key advantage of a quality artificial tree is its ability to support the weight of so many bulbs. A real tree of comparable height can handle about 800 bulbs. As a rule of thumb, I recommend using a minimum of 100

ABOVE LEFT: **Placed in a fiberglass urn that mimics rusted iron and surrounded by supersized sugar-pine cones, a blue spruce strikes an urbane pose: Witness the coppery globes, fresh Dendrobium orchids in florist's vials, sprays of dried hydrangea, and gold miniature lights. The drama continues with strings of bulbs forming a curtain of light behind translucent drapes.** ABOVE RIGHT: **A classic Radko tree is finished with a tree skirt based on an eight-pointed star — the symbol of the company.**

LIT FROM WITHIN

Not to be confused with electric bulbs, Dresden figurals are glass light covers. A threaded collar attaches to a lightbulb so that the bulb can be replaced when it burns out. My company is now making these charming light covers, which are entirely hand-painted, in a variety of designs adapted from among our most popular ornaments. Snowmen, candy canes, Santa, nutcrackers, even slices of cake glow with warmth. One of my personal favorites is a lighthouse that is, naturally, called "Night Light." You can also find faceted acrylic covers to fit over mini-lights to make them look the size of C-7s without the same output of heat.

lights for every foot of height.

Before you start, be sure to check all your strands of lights for worn electrical cords and replace any dead bulbs. Follow manufacturer's instructions regarding how many strands can be plugged together; six is the usual number. Always plug lights into a surge protector. Remove any tags on the lights after reading, and save them. It's a good idea to wear gloves, as real trees, particularly spruces, may have sharp needles, and an artificial tree will be coated with a fire retardant, which may irritate your skin.

Start a few inches above the base of the center pole or trunk, well away from the water bowl in the case of a real tree, and wrap around it several times to make the tree seem to glow from within. Then pull the lights out to the end of one of the branches on the lowest tier, running them under the branch. Work your way back along the branch, firmly wrapping the light cord around the branch and any strong offshoots or tips. On a natural tree, be careful not to wrap so tightly as to constrict the branches. When you get back to the trunk, repeat the process on another branch on the same tier, working up the tree. With an artificial tree that has sections, connect light strands so that they are self-contained in a section. For this reason and for general ease of use, I recommend using lights in strands of 50 rather than the more unwieldy 100.

For a heavily lit look, wrap all the branchettes; for a less intense look, skip the secondary branches or light every other one. After you have wrapped a small portion of the tree, step back and look at your handiwork. Now is the time to make any adjustments. Once you decide what degree of light you like, maintain that pattern. To achieve a consistent look, only one person should do the actual wrapping. A helper can come in handy, however, for unwrapping new lights, untangling old lights, testing each strand, and passing them to you. Count on about four hours for an 8-foot tree with 800 bulbs; 3,000 bulbs on an artificial tree could take a beginner eight to ten hours. This time commitment explains why florists may charge up to $30 or more per foot to light a tree.

Spacing between bulbs is another factor in determining a look. Strands are sold with bulbs 4, 6, 8, or 10 inches apart. The smaller the distance, the more intense the impression of light. Lights also come in

LEFT: **Recalling an unassuming Victorian tree, a white pine proudly displays its treasures of cookies, candy canes, and reproduction chromolith paper ornaments, as well as a delicate frosting of tinsel.** ABOVE FROM LEFT TO RIGHT: **"Pine Cone Santa" and "Winter Acorn" ornaments and faux oak leaves and berries lend rusticity; The White Rabbit worries that he may be "late for a very important date" and a clip-on balloon fills in a bare spot; three-dimensional vintage "Dresden" ornaments are made of gilded, pressed cardboard.** BELOW FROM LEFT TO RIGHT: **"Midnight Magic," "King of Joy," "Chapel Hill," and "Royal Tapestry" globes display the intricate detail typical of all Radko ornaments; costume-jewelry pearls serve as garlands; a Victorian-style paper cone holds sweets.**

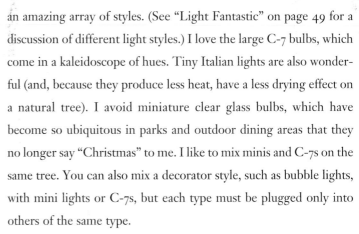

an amazing array of styles. (See "Light Fantastic" on page 49 for a discussion of different light styles.) I love the large C-7 bulbs, which come in a kaleidoscope of hues. Tiny Italian lights are also wonderful (and, because they produce less heat, have a less drying effect on a natural tree). I avoid miniature clear glass bulbs, which have become so ubiquitous in parks and outdoor dining areas that they no longer say "Christmas" to me. I like to mix minis and C-7s on the same tree. You can also mix a decorator style, such as bubble lights, with mini lights or C-7s, but each type must be plugged only into others of the same type.

Strands of lights are available in multicolor, single hues, and such combinations as red-and-white for a peppermint candy-cane effect, but you can create your own special and unique combinations with replacement bulbs. Purple, green, and gold lend a harlequin effect; red, white, and blue, a patriotic look. Or light the tree in one color, say, gold, then accent the tips of branches with red, for example.

I recommend using quality lights, such as those manufactured by GKI and other manufacturers that sell their products in Christmas stores and other high-end retailers, rather than those available only over the holidays in supermarkets and pharmacies. Quality lights burn reliably for years, meaning you don't have to replace individual bulbs as often. They also offer a greater palette of colors, and because bulbs are double-dipped, those colors are richer. Buy only light sets that are Underwriters Laboratories–approved, ensuring that the cord is insulated and the bulbs will not overheat. (Look for the UL hologram tag.) In the case of miniature lights, avoid straight-line construction. When one bulb burns out, all the rest go out. To be sure, look for three entwined cords. In the case of C-7s, you should be able to comfortably hold a lighted bulb in the palm of your hand for about a minute. If you can't remember when you bought a light set, it is probably time to replace it, since regulations have recently been tightened.

I've found even people who treat their ornaments like the crown jewels often don't give Christmas lights the respect they deserve. Think ahead when you take down your tree. If you just toss your light strings into a box willy-nilly, you'll waste hours untangling

OPPOSITE: **This extravaganza of a tree suggests a turn-of-the-19th-century Christmas.** ABOVE: **In the center of the tree, a Radko Neapolitan angel nestles in a halo of bows.** BELOW: **These antique German glass perfume bottles were sold with a cork and a hook to convert to Christmas ornaments after the scent was used up. The pot-metal reindeer are also German.**

RIGHT: **A balsam fir wears a variety of decorations, linked by a metallic color scheme. Glass globes pair with gilded faux leaves, silky upholstery tassels, and lametta tinsel stars. Tufts of coppery and bronzy angel hair and miniature chartreuse lights lend a warm glow. Swagged double strings of faux pearls, interspersed with garlands of lametta tinsel, provide an unconventional finishing touch.** BELOW: **Beneath the tree, an illuminated village is composed of reproductions of churches and houses made in Japan in the 1960s and now being made again for Radko. Lengths of damask and gauze anchor the composition.**

them a year later. Arrange them neatly on their holders and replace any burned-out lights so you'll be ready to go the following year.

Ornament Time

Now, at last, it's time to turn to the ornaments. Carefully remove their wrappings and lay them all out on a table. Check that the caps of glass ornaments are securely attached by the spring loop inside. If it has come loose, simply pull out the bent wire, being careful not to remove the cap or crown, then reshape the circle at the top and spread out the spring like a wishbone. Pinch it closed and reinsert it in the crown. It should be nice and tight again. (Remove hangers before storing; glass ornaments with hooks could scratch delicate painted surfaces.)

Make sure you have a good supply of quality ornament hangers with a loop at either end, allowing you to secure the hanger snugly to both the ornament and the branch. Dark green hangers blend into the foliage. Avoid small, flimsy hangers that cannot support much weight and may slip off the branch. Lightweight, shiny holders tend to stick together when you try to grab one. Also have on hand a supply of green florist's wire for securing larger ornaments. Attach ornament holders to lighter ornaments, being careful not to scratch the surface. Cut six-inch lengths of florist's wire with a wire cutter and set aside.

If your tree is taller than seven feet, make sure you have a stable ladder at the ready. A footstool should serve for shorter trees. A helper who can pass you ornaments is useful, especially if you are standing on a ladder. Start with your tree topper. If you have trouble getting the finial to sit tightly and vertically on top of the tree, wrap the growing tip with aluminum foil for added thickness. Or if the tip is too short, extend it by wiring on a piece of wood dowel.

Now you're ready to proceed with the rest of the decorating. (If you did not wrap lights around the trunk or pole, wrap tinsel garlands around it.) If you'll be using glass garlands, place them first, before attaching any ornaments. Divide the tree into three zones and the ornaments into two groups. For a balanced look, you'll want to put the smallest ornaments at the top of the tree and the largest ones at the bottom, blending the sizes in the middle. This assumes

---

UNDERNEATH IT ALL

Imagine getting all dressed up to go out and forgetting to put on your shoes. Unless you are lucky enough to have an attractive antique tree stand that is worth showing off, a tree skirt or other fabric treatment gives a decorated tree a finished look and protects gifts and little fingers from sticky resin.

Another approach is to place the tree in an attractive container. This approach often works best with small or tabletop trees. You may be able to rig up a tree stand within the container; if not, you'll have to rely on stones or pea gravel to stabilize the tree. Also, be sure to consider how you will keep the tree hydrated. If your container is waterproof, all the better. If it is not, make sure that you can fit a container for water inside the decorative container. Consider these possibilities:

- A metal or fiberglass decorative planter (be sure to weight fiberglass so it will not tip over)
- A large terra-cotta pot, perhaps treated for a mossy look
- A large glazed planter or Chinese fishbowl
- A big basket, such as an apple-picking or laundry basket
- A woven hamper

LEFT: **This soldier toy hails from the Erzgebirge region of Germany, known for quality wooden toys and Christmas decorations. The latticework device aligns the figures in a variety of marching positions.**
BELOW LEFT: **Decoratively wrapped presents feature small added gifts that hint at the contents.** BELOW: **Three doubled-sided Santas on the circa-1904 German tree stand are lithographed onto tin. The German art glass golden-lacquered deer were blown freeform between 1910 and 1930.**

A Douglas fir is dressed with silvery jingle bells, some made into roping, and GKI mini-lights in a color combination of gold, purple, chartreuse, and red designed by Christopher Radko and called "Imperiale." The swagged garlands reiterate the shape of the gingerbread trim on the porch. The staircase and railing wear greens decorated with lights and bells.

that you have no other considerations, such as small children or rambunctious pets, requiring only unbreakable ornaments below a certain level. I like to hang plain colored balls on the inside of the tree, where they will hide the trunk and reflect light, saving the more prominent spots on the outside for figural ornaments. However, if you have only a few figurals, you may want to intersperse them with globes on the outside of the tree. I believe in decorating all the way around the tree to give a sense of fullness. On the less visible side of the tree, you can stick older, even broken ornaments or those to which you have a sentimental attachment but which may no longer meet your aesthetic standards.

Start at the top of the tree so that you will not brush against ornaments already in place. Then place your favorite and most beautiful ornaments where they are most visible. Ornaments should hang down from the branch, rather than rest on foliage, for a graceful look. Carefully secure each ornament to a tree branch before moving on to the next. Then fill in with other ornaments, always striving for a balanced look. Clip-on ornaments that sit above branches also work well on the top third of the tree. From time to time step back and regard your handiwork from several vantage points.

As you move into the middle portion of the tree, start interspersing the occasional large ornament. As you approach the bottom third, you should have used up most of your smaller ornaments. To hang the heavier glass ornaments and those made of metal, wood, or other heavy materials, you'll most likely have to use florist's wire. Wrap one end through the spring hood at the top of the ornament, making a loop about two inches long. Then wrap the other end of the wire around the branch a few times in a corkscrew motion, leaving about a quarter inch between the branch and the ornament. Be careful not to overlap the wire; spread it out so that when you take down the tree, you can pull it off the branch without having to unwind it. Wind each wire clockwise around each branch, then simply go counterclockwise when you remove them. Or simply use a wire cutter to snip the quarter-inch piece of wire, being careful to support the ornament with your other hand. Don't try this technique on an artificial tree where you might mistakenly snip the wire framework of the tree. Here's another insiders' trick: Hot-gluing will diminish the value of collectible ornaments, but does ensure that a delicate glass globe will not detach from its holder and fall to the floor.

For the birds, a living tree tempts with birdseed ornaments and petite pepperberry wreaths.

All the Extras

If you have lightweight garlands or plan to use only a few glass garlands, you can add them once your ornaments are in place. Radko glass garlands come with a hook at either end, making it easy to attach them to a branch or to each other. For extra security, wire each hook to a branch. Use floral wire each time you swag a garland. Large beads lend themselves to wide swags; smaller beads offer more flexibility. The trick is to drape them in loose, relaxed-looking shapes. If they are too tightly swagged, garlands lose their wonderful curviness. You can achieve different looks ranging from an informal free-form treatment to a very symmetrical, swagged effect. Or,

The traditional date for taking down your Christmas decorations is January 6, known as Twelfth Night. Many cultures consider it bad luck to leave greens in the house after that date. Whenever you decide it's time to pack it all away for hibernation, follow a few guidelines to minimize the mess, protect your ornaments, and make setup easier next year:

Use a rigid box with dividers (so ornaments do not rub against one another) to store your holiday treasures. You can use the lightweight boxes that some ornaments are sold in within the rigid box, but don't rely on them alone to protect ornaments. Some boxes are made of acid-free cardboard, but this is not necessary for the regular collector as long as you wrap delicate ornaments in acid-free paper. Hard plastic boxes may seal too tightly, trapping moisture that could damage delicate lacquer finishes. Some plastics also off-gas chemicals that could be toxic. Never wipe mouth-blown glass ornaments with water or cleanser. The delicate paints could run or be otherwise damaged. Instead, dust them lightly with a clean feather duster.

Proper packing materials provide an extra measure of protection. Acid-free tissue, Bounty microwave paper towels (the only brand that's acid free), and all-cotton fabric are ideal. Never wrap ornaments in plastic or bubble wrap for the reasons listed above. Newspaper is also a no-no because the ink can transfer to and stain the surface of ornaments. Store your ornaments in a place in the house where the temperature is reasonably stable. Extremes of heat and cold, likely in a basement, attic, or garage, can cause painted surfaces to flake. A closet in living quarters is an ideal location.

Check light strings for burned-out bulbs and replace them. If you are not leaving them on an artificial tree, replace them in their original containers so they will not get tangled up. If you have misplaced the boxes and plastic inserts, wrap each string around a shirt cardboard and secure with masking tape or twist ties. Or plug the two ends of a light set together like a snake biting its tail, then loop it into a neat circle.

---

connect garlands and spiral them from the top of the tree down and around, graduating from those with smaller beads to ones with larger beads. You could even wrap a small tree completely in garlands. While my favorite garlands are made of glass, strings of tiny pinecones, dime-store pearls, and other materials also lend themselves to garlands.

Ribbons can be the perfect finishing touch on a tree. If you have only a modest collection of ornaments, ribbons can also enhance the impression of abundance. Ribbon comes in a wondrous array of types, colors, and patterns, ranging from rustic raffia to elegant gold braid. Tie small bows to the end of tree branches, or at the top of each ornament or every other ornament. Make larger bows and attach them like ornaments strategically around the tree. Tie long lengths of satin ribbon to the top of the tree, then swirl it around for a maypole effect. Tie jingle bells or tiny ornaments to the ribbon ends.

I love the retro look of tinsel, which is enjoying a renewed popularity. Like the custom of decorating a Christmas tree and the manufacture of blown-glass ornaments, tinsel was invented in Germany—way back around 1610!—although German folklore holds that the first tinsel was actually made from spiderwebs. Originally a machine pulled real silver into wafer-thin strips. Today, most tinsel is made of Mylar or cellophane. (If you have pets, play it safe and forgo the tinsel, which can cause serious problems if swallowed.)

Like the garnish on a cake, tinsel is the last thing you put on a tree. For a truly magical effect, place each strand individually so that it hangs vertically, just as a real icicle would. Tinsel comes in a variety of metallic hues, and even several colors. Lametta, tufted tinsel attached to a strand of twisted wires or thread, is the Rolls-Royce of tinsel. Made the same way for more than 150 years, it is imported from Germany. The copper wire is flattened and silver-plated for a mellow luster that adds a nostalgic, luminous look to any tree.

Lametta comes in various widths and styles and even several colors. Lametta garlands with a thread core drape beautifully.

Tinsel's cousin, aptly named angel hair (*Engelshaar* in German), also supplies an Old World look. Made of spun glass, it, too, comes in a variety of shades from white to gold to bronze. Puffs of angel hair in the center of the tree soften the silhouettes of the branches, add their own glow, and softly diffuse electric lights.

When it comes to Christmas trees, if you can imagine it, you can pretty much create it. The options available for decorating the tree are enormous and the

Light up the night:
A summery gazebo does a winter turn with a cut spruce tree decorated with multicolor globes from the Radko Accents collection and multiple strings of mini-lights. More lights trace the graceful lines of the structure.

looks you can achieve, equally varied. But instead of being intimidated by this plethora of choices, go with your instincts. For one time during the year, forget about the taste police. There is always a place for a little tackiness. As legendary *Vogue* editor Diana Vreeland once said, "Good taste is a bore." Whatever you love is fine and however you want to combine your ornaments is up to you.

You may also want a theme to your tree. For an updated Colonial Williamsburg look, for example, hang glass ornaments that rival real apples, pears, plums, strawberries, and other fruits. Intersperse traditional cranberries or popcorn with shiny golden beads for an unusual garland treatment, and use lights that look like real candles. If you want a superurbane look, you might try using masses of tiny chartreuse lights, silvery icicles, and colored balls.

To paraphrase Will Rogers, I've rarely met an ornament I didn't like. Even homemade ornaments have their own sweet appeal. Be especially respectful of the ornaments your parents and grandparents passed down to you. These fragile trinkets are tangible evidence of their lives—memories caught in the glitter of glass. Tree toppers, lights, ornaments, garlands, ribbons, tinsel, and angel hair are all the standards of Christmas-tree décor, but don't stop with them. Play with feathers, decorated cookies, upholstery tassels, crystal chandelier drops, costume jewelry, toys, small pieces of crochet, and silk and even fresh flowers. That way, your tree can be as individual as you are.

The Finishing Touch

Now step back and admire your handiwork, make any needed adjustments, and—unless your tree is in an urn or other decorative container—add a tree skirt. After all, the well-dressed tree needs to be decorated from tip to toe. You can purchase many attractive tree skirts or make your own out of velvet, satin, wool tartan, felt or another fabric. Or you can simply drape such materials around the base of the tree in a pleasing fashion. Because a tree skirt is basically a circle with a hole cut in the middle, you may find it makes it easier to keep the tree hydrated than when using bunched fabric. A few overlapping sheepskins at the base of the tree not only suggest snow, their softness cushions a falling ornament. Other options include cotton batting that emulates snow, a buffalo-plaid blanket, or even a patchwork quilt. To prevent damage to fabrics, put a piece of plastic shower curtain or other protective material between the tree base and your temporary tree skirt. It also is a good idea to put a cushion of cotton batting underneath the tree skirt to cushion any falling ornaments.

Unless it is surrounded by presents, a tree can look rather lonely in the weeks before the big day. Strew large pinecones around the base or arrange pots of poinsettias, a collection of Santa figures, nutcrackers, or other collectibles. Of course, for many of us, a Christmas tree just isn't complete without an electric train—and its corresponding miniature alpine village—chugging around. Now, that's what Christmas is all about!

Small is beautiful. OPPOSITE: **A Lilliputian feather tree decorated with tiny red glass globes is the centerpiece of an arrangement with a hunting theme. Red and green plates and a small painting celebrate riding to the hounds; the golden beaded lamp shades add another festive touch.** BELOW: **Burlap balls make these tiny artificial trees look almost real.**

BURNING BRIGHT

PARTNERS IN BEAUTY, glass Christmas ornaments bask in the reflected glow of electric lights. Today there are hundreds of decorative options that harmonize with glass and other ornaments. And outdoors, where they can hog the spotlight, electrified ornaments come into their own.

Decades of Light

Thomas Edison invented the electric lightbulb in 1879; and in 1882, the first tree decorated with lights (blinking, and with red, white, and blue bulbs, no less) appeared in the home of Edward H. Johnson, then the vice president of Edison's electric light company. But as they did with ornaments, the Germans were the first to make Christmas lights into an industry. Austria and Hungary soon joined in, as did some American companies. The first bulbs manufactured in the 1890s were either simple globes or shaped like pears or flames. They were made of clear glass painted in various colors, while more expensive lights were made of tinted glass. Figural lightbulbs shaped into forms similar to those used for glass ornaments followed in 1908. Subjects included bells, birds, fruits, flowers, Kewpie dolls, clowns, Santa, and such nursery-rhyme characters as Humpty-Dumpty and Mother Goose. Betty Boop, Moon Mullins, and other cartoon characters were also popular, including Walt Disney's characters. By the 1920s, the Japanese had gotten into the act. Until this time

Lessons in Light

To make illumination more than just an afterthought to ornaments, use as many bulbs as the tree can handle and follow these tips:

• • •

Use two or three different sizes of bulbs, which will give a look of greater depth and rhythm.

• • •

Mix clear and frosted lights for a depth of effect.

• • •

Instead of clear glass bulbs, which can look harsh against green foliage, use chartreuse, which plays nicely off it.

• • •

Use replacement bulbs to create your own signature color mixes.

• • •

Use specialty bulbs such as bubble lights or snowballs in addition to standard C-7s or miniature lights.

LEFT: **Two strawlike rayon trees from the 1950s display bubble lights of the era. The center tree's Matchless Stars were made in the 1930s of Czechoslovakian cut crystal.** FOLLOWING PAGE, TOP TO BOTTOM: **Acrylic starburst novelty lights by GKI only look like crystal; vintage bubble lights and paper Whirl-Glo shades complement the celluloid reindeer, crocheted snowflakes, and other memorabilia.**

many families continued to use candles on their trees, either because they did not have electricity or because they mistrusted or could not afford the newfangled electric lights.

By the mid-1920s, figural lights had had their heyday, and the most common Christmas lights to be found were the simple cone-shaped bulbs in various colors. Metal-foil-covered cardboard or steel reflectors shaped like stars or flowers enhanced their effect. Twinkle lights appeared in the 1930s, as did Whirl-Glo shades, which were made of treated paper, which twirled around fanned by the heat generated by the bulb, combining motion and color to hypnotic effect. Matchless Stars, imported from Czechoslovakia, surrounded a bulb with one or two rows of col-

Outside Options

Exterior lighting has gained popularity in recent years with numerous products to stimulate your creativity. In addition to C-7s, which can be used indoors or out, the larger, flame-shaped C-9s are designed for outdoor use, as are certain miniature lights. Make sure that any lights you use outdoors are intended for that purpose.

Vintage or Reproduction Lights

Tell me what lights were on your childhood tree and I can probably guess your age to within a few years. If you hanker, say, after the bubble lights you loved as a kid, one option is to check out antique dealers and those who specialize in Christmas memorabilia, as well as eBay. However, using these vintage strings has its dangers. Old electrical cords may be frayed and connections broken. Unplug vintage lights when you cannot keep an eye on them. Today, the general mood of nostalgia has generated numerous reproductions; Radko is now selling bubble lights as part of its Memories line. So you can get the vintage look without paying collectors' prices or making any sacrifice in safety.

ored cut-crystal prisms that shimmered like precious jewels. Bubble lights, which are filled with colored liquid and a chemical that causes the contents to bubble with warmth rather like a Lava lamp, appeared in the 1940s. A postwar phenomenon, fluorescent lights were a fleeting fad. Increasingly, bulbs were made of plastic, among them the star-shaped Wonder Lights.

Miniature lights, hailing from Italy, appeared in the 1950s. The bright dots of light revolutionized the look of Christmas trees. Although the first miniature lights were of clear glass, soon they were being made in several colors, most could be made to flash on and off. Up to that time strings of lights had included perhaps twelve bulbs. Suddenly, strings of 35, 50, even 100 were commonplace.

Light Fantastic

Although clear white miniature lights dominated the market for several decades, today colored lights are increasing in popularity, and that couldn't make me happier.

My preference is to use as much color as possible to enhance the magical effect. In addition to the expected red, blue, green, and yellow, lights come in teal, pink, purple, gold, and other hues. Some miniature bulbs are designed to twinkle. I prefer those that come on slowly until they achieve a lovely glow then fade off equally slowly, rather than those that flash on and off like a neon sign in an all-night diner.

And Christmas lights are once more available in splendid variety. The traditional C-7s, which now use only six volts of electricity, come in transparent, opaque, and satin finishes. Novelty sets include chili peppers, pinecones, berries, clusters of grapes, beaded fruit, horses, angels, Santa, snowmen, tiny gift boxes, and even nutcrackers. For the icy glow of the northern lights, look for acrylic bulbs in the shape of stars, icicles, snowflakes, chunks of "crystal," or snowballs. Tiny metal lanterns, tin bells with cutouts, clip-on "candles," crystal-look votives holding tiny electric candles, and poinsettia or magnolia blooms that surround a bulb fall into the category of lighted ornaments.

For all their glittering magic, Christmas lights do pose hazards if used improperly. Here's how to keep your family safe.

• Check all electric lights and connections before decorating. Don't use lights with worn or frayed cords or missing or broken bulbs. Make sure the lights and cords are UL-approved.

• Use surge protectors and don't overload electrical outlets. Use no more than three sets of lights per extension cord.

• Don't place cords under rugs or in where someone could trip over them.

• Turn off the lights when you leave the room. Unplug the lights if you leave the house.

WINTER WONDERLAND

WHETHER WE LIVE IN COLORADO OR FLORIDA, WE
SHARE A COLLECTIVE VISION OF CHRISTMAS,
COMPLETE WITH COLORFUL LIGHTS GLIMMERING ON
PERFECTLY PYRAMIDAL TREES. A FRESH SNOWFALL
ADDING ITS OWN SOFTNESS AND SPARKLE IS ESSENTIAL
TO THIS FANTASY. THE BEAUTY OF SNOW TOUCHES US
ON SOME PROFOUND LEVEL. GERMAN AND DUTCH
FAIRY TALES DESCRIBE SNOWFLAKES AS FEATHERS
BEING SHAKEN FROM HER FEATHERBED BY HOLLE, THE
QUEEN OF WINTER. I LOVE TO SEE A PINE BRANCH
HEAVY WITH SNOW, ITS FROSTY BLANKET PERFECTLY
BALANCED ON THE BOUGH. WHEN I SEE TREES
GROANING UNDER THE WEIGHT OF SNOW, IT REMINDS
ME OF POSTCARDS FROM THE 1930S DEPICTING
EUROPEAN SKI RESORTS.

ou may not be able to guarantee snow for the holidays, but at the very moment when nature goes into hibernation you can do a myriad of other things to give the exterior of your house some Christmas magic. As a bonus, you will lift the spirits of every passerby.

In all your outdoor efforts, take your cues from the habits of living plants as well as the architectural lines of your house. Unleash your creativity by accenting foundation plantings with lights and decorating architectural details with cut greenery, berries, pinecones, and weatherproof ribbon. On a porch protected from the elements, you might even be able to include some glass ornaments. Add atmosphere with oil lamps or lanterns. For a spectacular fire-and-ice effect, place candles in homemade ice votives. Lining a pathway or gracing a set of steps, they twinkle invitingly.

Don't overlook old sleds, toboggans, wooden skis, straps of sleigh bells, snowshoes, and other objects that are the hallmarks of an old-fashioned Christmas. Check out the barn or the attic for such props, or pick them up during the summer at tag sales when no one else is interested. Your goal is to create a winter fantasyland, but be careful not to step over the line into kitsch, unless that's the look you're after.

If your indoor Christmas tree can be seen from the front of the house, play it up on the exterior with a frame of lights and greenery. In addition to wreaths in the windows or swagged evergreens over the top, you might want to fill window boxes with evergreens or moss topiaries, or even tiny Christmas trees. You need not decorate every window; instead, perhaps accent just a pair of bay windows or an oval powder-room window. Again, knowing when to stop is as important as not being too cautious.

Nature's Gifts

Plantings around your house lend themselves to Christmas decorating two ways: first, as opportunities to accent them with lights and other decorations, and second,

PREVIOUS PAGE: **Garlands of greenery, planters overflowing with juniper, baby eucalyptus and birch branches, votive lights in sand-filled buckets, and lights galore signal welcome.** ABOVE: **An Appalachian split-ash backpack holds a spray of mixed greens.** OPPOSITE: **Bringing home a cut tree is an age-old ritual.**

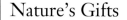

as materials to cut selectively for use both indoors and out. As a gardener, I am always conscious of creating a four-season garden. Evergreens are the backbone of any garden because their beauty is not confined to one or two seasons. In fact, they—and particularly living topiaries—become even more beautiful when dusted with snow. (A heavy snowfall can damage delicate branches and should be removed promptly and as completely as possible.) Consider including some white pines, blue spruces, arborvitae, boxwood, or spiral junipers or other ornamental evergreens around the front of your house. Each has a distinctive shape and some ornamentals are bred to have a weeping or otherwise unusual profile. Unlike standard specimens, dwarf varieties will not overpower the house within a few seasons.

Pick evergreens with interesting cones—some are furry, some long and skinny, others short and squat, some green, some silvery, others brown—that will add another element of beauty to the garden after fall's chrysanthemums have blackened with frost. Evergreens also lend themselves beautifully to illumination. And lest we forget our feathered friends, evergreens provide undergrowth that offers birds nesting places and protection from the elements. Also, plant trees and shrubs whose leaves will turn brilliant colors or bear colorful twigs or berries when most of Nature is dressed in drab. Among my favorites are Japanese barberry, winterberry, pepperberry, privet, pyracantha, juniper, holly, and dogwood.

PERFECT PINECONES

As anyone who has struggled to tell one species of evergreen from another knows, the answer lies in the cones. The term "pinecone" (scientific name, *Pinaceae*) is used for all conifers (cone bearers), including hemlocks, spruces, larches, firs, and Douglas fir. Although all pinecones share basically the same construction of overlapping rows of scales spiraling around a central axis, each species is remarkably different in size and shape. The Papa Bear of the pinecone is that of the sugar pine, whose cylindrical, blunt-pointed cones can be as long as 18 inches. The white pine's similarly shaped cones tend to be 5 to 9 inches long. Pinyon pinecones range from $1^1/_2$ to 3 inches in length. The longleaf, slash, and Jeffrey pines, in contrast, have more egg-shaped cones with the base significantly larger than the tip. Spruce, hemlock, and larch all have much smaller cones, some less than an inch in length.

If boughs of greens come with cones attached, you're in luck. If not, you can go Mother Nature one better and wire on any cones you desire. Or wire bases of cones together to make a cluster before adding to your arrangement. You can also make wreaths and garlands solely from pinecones. If stored carefully, they should last for several seasons.

Raw Materials

The same plantings that make your property attractive provide a free source of foliage for wreaths and other decorations. There is nothing like being able to go out your front door, pruning shears in hand, and return with armfuls of boughs

TAKE YOUR PICK

MANY EVERGREENS, such as pines and firs, bear needlelike leaves. Some, such as junipers, are made up on scales; other species have larger, flat leaves that persist through the winter.

ATLAS CEDAR (*Cedrus atlantica*): The blue-green or silvery short needles contrast nicely with dark green or yellow-green plants.

BAY (*Laurus nobilis*): As the fragrant, elliptical, pointed leaves of grayish green, dry, they curl slightly. Use by itself in wreaths or garlands or mix with needled plants.

BOXWOOD (*Buxaceae*): The small, shiny leaves are ideal for garlands. Use it at its freshest, for greater flexibility.

DEODAR CEDAR (*C. deodara*): Known as the California Christmas tree, its needles are darker green than the atlas cedar, which also has small, barrel-shaped cones.

CYPRESS (*Cyressus*): Depending upon the species, the conelike fruit may be dull purple or grayish blue.

Its color and texture contrast nicely with conventional evergreens.

GALAX (*Galax aphylla*): The heart shape of galax leaves adds interest to mixed wreaths. They take on an attractive bronze tint in autumn.

HEMLOCK (*Tsuga*): This conifer has delicate, dark green needles and equally small cones.

IVY (*Hedera*): This vine lends itself to wreaths, garlands, and kissing balls.

JUNIPER (*Juniperus*): There are numerous varieties of junipers, but all are aromatic, and the spiky foliage is made up of scales rather than needles. Small berries nestle in the leaves, some blue kissed with a powdery haze; others are closer to silver in hue.

LAUREL: With its pointed leaves, laurel makes lovely wreaths and garlands alone or in combination with needled evergreens. Laurel comprises several genera, including mountain laurel (*Kalmia latifolia*), which is a protected species in some states.

MAGNOLIA (*Magnoliaceae*): The long-lasting green leaves have rust-brown backs. Their leathery texture lends itself to being stapled to a wreath form or other shapes.

MISTLETOE (*Phoradendron*): The waxy leaves of mistletoe dry within a week to a chartreuse color. The berries are poisonous. Don't limit your use of mistletoe to kissing balls. It makes a handsome wreath or garland. Just be sure to work with it when it is still fresh enough to adapt to the desired shape. Use tight, compact clusters for a lush look.

FROM LEFT TO RIGHT: **Laurel, boxwood, galax, bay, and olive.**

OLIVE AND RUSSIAN OLIVE (*Oltea*): Both have pointed leaves, similar in shape to bay, but smaller. The backs of the leaves are distinctly silvery.

OREGON GRAPE (*Mahonia aquifolium*): This evergreen shrub sports blue berries.

PACHYSANDRA: This common, glossy green ground cover can make wonderful garlands.

PINE (*Pinus*): White pine is probably the most common holiday green, with soft and pliant boughs with a floppy look. One caution: White pine dries out quickly, although this is less of a problem outdoors. Pine roping can be made more interesting by interweaving other greens of contrasting colors and textures.

PRINCESS PINE (*Lycopdium*): Not a true pine, this club moss has a petite scale and lacy look that make it perfect for small creations. In some areas, princess pine is endangered.

PRIVET (*Ligustrum*): One of the classic shrubs for live topiaries, privet has a small, glossy green leaf and green berries that open to turn purple-blue.

CLOCKWISE FROM TOP LEFT: **Yew, juniper, Carolina Sapihira, cypress, Deodar cedar, Atlas cedar, and rosemary.**

EUCALYPTUS: This native of Australia comes in numerous varieties. The leaves may be pointed, oblate, or even rounded, but all are aromatic and smoky blue-green in color. Some have seedpods attached.

FALSE CYPRESS (*Crippsii*): This feathery chartreuse green holds up well for weeks.

and berries for making your own wreaths or other arrangements. Depending upon your locale, look for inspiration in other native plants such as ears of dried Indian corn, autumn leaves, ferns, sheaves of rice or wheat, cotton bolls, or horse chestnuts. I can't think of a more personal gift than a wreath made from plants grown in your own garden. You actually have far more options with outside decorations, where cuttings will last considerably longer than inside a heated house.

By the way, once they are well established, most shrubs and trees benefit from judicious pruning, coming back even fuller. The exception is evergreens with needles: Boughs will not grow back once cut to the trunk, so concentrate on pruning smaller offshoots. You may also want to swap greens with friends and neighbors: for example, some boughs of holly in return for a basket of balsam. Depending on your region, there are numerous other options. Southerners can take advantage of magnolia and camellia leaves; residents of the Northwest can turn to cedar sprays, Oregon grape, and salal leaves. A walk in the woods can also prove profitable. In the Hudson River valley, near the Radko offices, a vine called bittersweet attachs itself to trees and

shrubs. As the days shorten, yellow berries appear, then burst to reveal their crimson centers. I always gather a wiry bunch to tuck into garlands and weave into wreaths.

If your property or surrounding countryside doesn't lend itself to a cutting garden or you want foliage you don't grow or that isn't native to your area, you have plenty of other options—although none so cost-effective! The downtown parking lot that offers Christmas trees often also has some of the more basic greens in garland, spray, and wreath form. If they're fresh—be sure to get there early—you can often personalize them with such adornments as ribbons, pinecones, berries, and weatherproof ornaments. Tree farms sometimes broaden their inventory to include greenery, and many florists carry a good array of greenery at holiday season. It's a good idea to check with one or more florists well before the holidays to get an idea of what they are likely to have, and to reserve what you need.

Another source of swags, wreaths, sprays, and other greenery are mail-order

OPPOSITE: **A pair of spiral "wobblers" placed in urns tied with bunches of raffia bear candles and vines of Canadian bittersweet. A spray of ivy and other greens tied with more raffia on the door and a cast stone squirrel hint at the delights within.**
ABOVE: **A lush garland of variegated holly with berries, juniper, pine, and balsam fir is illuminated with both electric bulbs and votive candles in ice holders.**

BERRY PRETTY

An accent of color may start with holly berries, but it certainly doesn't end there. The following plants have handsome berries that make them good landscaping choices for winter display as well as raw material for wreaths and other arrangements. You can also use branches of not-yet-ripe persimmons, pomegranates, figs, crab apples, pears, quince, or even grapes.

ANDROMEDA includes several shrubs in the heather family, which have a spiky growth and green and pink berries.

BAYBERRY (*Myrica caroliniensis*) bears tiny, silver-blue, waxy berries with a hazy bloom that gives them a pastel effect. The waxy coating on the resinous berries is used for making candles.

CLOCKWISE FROM TOP LEFT: **Nandina domestica, euca-lyptus, pink pepperberries, pyracantha, winter-berry, bittersweet, and pittosporum.**

BEAUTY-BERRY (*Callicarpa*) bears its bright red berries skewerlike on twigs after the deciduous leaves have dropped.

BITTERSWEET (*Celastrus scandens*) has yellow-orange berries split open to reveal their red hearts. The vine habit makes it ideal for loose wreaths; soaking them makes it easier to coax them into shape. Another vine with green berries (*Solanum dulcama*) is called Canadian bittersweet.

CHINESE TALLOW TREE (*Sapium sebiferum*) offers opaque white berries.

EUCALYPTUS SEEDPODS come in various shapes and colors. Some are warty capsules shaped like tops or stars, others a group of hanging elliptical berries. The color ranges from silvery to chartreuse.

EUONYMUS has white berries that split open to reveal bright orange-red centers.

HAWTHORN (*Crataegus*) comes in numerous varieties of leaf size and shape, but always carries glossy red berries.

LEUCADENDRON has showy conelike berries that, depending upon variety, may be red, silver, white, or brown.

NANDINA DOMESTICA displays crimson berries whose color is echoed in red-tipped leaves.

PEPPERBERRY (*Shinus terebinthifolius*) has green ripening to pink or red berries, depending upon variety, which are densely bunched, suggesting lush, free-form uses.

PITTOSPORUM bears small, oval leaves with relatively large berries that start out the color of a Granny Smith apple and ripen to yellow and orange. They can be striking in an all-berry wreath.

PYRACANTHA is known as fire thorn for its dense bunches of bold orange-red or yellow berries and thorny branches. The small-leafed foliage is glossy green.

ROSE HIPS (*Rosa*) are the fruit that follows the bloom of a rose. Born on unruly vines, the bright red hips come in various sizes depending on the variety of rose. If you want their showy look for decorations, do not deadhead your roses.

ROSEMARY (*Rosmarinus officinalis*): A woody shrub that is an ideal plant for interior decorations. It's aroma comes from resinous oils.

SALAL (*Gaultheria shallon*), a relative of wintergreen, bears purple berries.

SMILAX bears tiny blue-black berries on thorny stems.

SNOWBERRY (*Symphoricarpos albus*) is named for its globular white fruits.

SPRUCE (*Picea*): A classic choice for Christmas trees, spruce is actually better suited for outdoor use as the needles drop quickly as it dries out. Blue spruce offers nice color contrast to other greens but the sharp needles make it hard to work with. Be sure to wear heavy gloves.

STRAWBERRY TREE (*Arbutus unedo*), as the common name indicates, bears large, warty, yellow to red fruits that look vaguely like strawberries. The tough-skinned berries dry well.

SUMAC (*Rhus*): Long after its leaves have turned crimson and fallen to the ground, sumac displays velvety red or pale berries borne at the end of thick, woody stalks. An evergreen variety is native to the West Coast.

TOYON (*Heteromeles arbutifolia*), also known as Christmas holly or Christmas berry, is a shrub native to California. The red fruit, which grow in profusion and look like miniature apples, and evergreen foliage make it popular for Christmas decorations.

VIBURNUM displays shiny blue berries and small green leaves on red stalks, making this a highly decorative plant.

WINTERBERRY (*Ilex verticulate*) The classic red berry seen on many wreaths is actually a deciduous holly.

YEW (*Taxus*): The dark green foliage and red fruits are attractive but the berries are highly poisonous so its use should be confined to landscaping.

catalogs and online resources. These often have the advantage of regional offerings not available locally. A brief Internet search for the phrase "Christmas greenery" turned up hundreds of vendors offering everything from freeze-dried fall foliage woven into garlands to eucalyptus wreaths and balsam swags. Here are just a few of my favorites:

- Flying Cloud Christmas Wreaths & Swags (*wreaths/frame.xmaswreaths.html*) grows holly, noble fir, juniper, incense cedar, boxwood, and pine.
- Gardeners Eden (800-822-9600; fax: 573-581-7361) lives up to its name with a superb selection of evergreen wreaths, garlands, living plants, and other items.
- Smith & Hawken (800-940-1170; *www.smithandhawken.com*) has a wonderful selection of traditional and unusual plant materials in wreaths, garlands, and many other shapes.
- Sunrise Country Evergreens (800-543-9828) offers wreaths, kissing balls, roping, and other decorations made from balsam fir.

Although you certainly can make your own garlands and wreaths (many magazines and Web sites offer instructions), a more time-effective treatment is to embellish ready-made models. Dress up an artificial garland, for example, with cut greens and berries, hiding its humble origins.

I am a big proponent of blending different greens for textural and color interest. Think of making wreaths, sprays, and garlands as you would a floral arrangement. Tulips alone are beautiful, but they become far more interesting when paired with daffodils, narcissus, and grape hyacinth. Similarly, a garland combining bay, noble fir, and juniper plays the leafy bay off the spiky needles of the fir and the scaly juniper foliage. Bring color into play as well. A berry wreath of fire-engine-red hawthorns and rose hips, crab apples kissed with yellow, and green pittosporum is far more dynamic than a wreath made from a single plant. Or experiment with scent: Rosemary, bay, and eucalyptus could make an aromatic welcome in a wreath hung on your kitchen door.

One of the clear distinctions between a professional and an amateur is an

Pepperberries, holly, hypericum, and twists of curly willow tuck into a wire wreath covered with moss. The various textures and colors play off a masonry chimney.

Branches of white-sprayed birch, boughs of juniper, and stalks of wheat spill from urns. Radko "Native Blend" corn ornaments nestle in the foliage. "Sugar Plums" and "Winter Acorns" grace the garland wrapped around the door frame. The porch floor is carpeted with balsam boughs.

understanding of the importance of scale. The most common error in any décor project is reticence or moderation. If you're not sure whether something is large enough or lush enough, you can pretty well assume it isn't. Another rule of thumb: If one is good, two or more are better, whether you're talking about wreaths, topiaries, or lanterns. It is also essential to go with the flow when it comes to greenery. If a plant's habit is soft and floppy, like most pines, for example, it lends itself naturally to draping, flowing treatments. On the other hand, boxwood is an example of a plant that tends to be rather stiff, especially when wired in a garland.

Fill In the Lines

When deciding what to decorate, look beyond the obvious. Do you have a gazebo in the garden? An arbor for climbing roses? A well house? A dramatic eave over the garage doors? Don't forget the lamppost or other outdoor lighting fixtures, even the mailbox. How about a birdhouse, a log pile, a wooden swing, a birdbath? A bench that hosts geraniums come spring might be the perfect perch for a graceful arrangement of pine boughs and large pinecones. Contemplate how any one of these features might be adorned with greenery. If nothing sparks your imagination, take a look at some garden-supply catalogs that offer attractive arches, trellises, topiary forms, and wire spirals that are as well suited to Christmas greenery (with or without lights) as they are to training live plants.

Marking the transition between the outside world and the inner sanctum of family life, your front door deserves special treatment. At the very least, invest in a well-proportioned wreath, or two if you have double doors. Or hang a spray on the door itself and place wreaths to either side or trace the doorframe in a compatible garland. As the focal point of the house, an entry that personifies the abundance of the season will lift your spirits—as well as your guests'—every time you come into the house.

Another classic look is to place a wreath in every window facing the street.

Multiples always have a dramatic impact, but this sight is not just aesthetically pleasing, it actually tugs at my heartstrings. Here are some other suggestions for the front door:

- Affix a demilune Della Robbia arrangement of pineapple (a traditional symbol of welcome), apples, and other freeze-dried or artificial fruit over the top of the door. Below, hang a wreath made from just one or two of the fruits.

- Wrap a door like a giant present in a sheet of red or silver Mylar. You can buy the wrap in crafts and Christmas stores, then add a big bow and top with a lush wreath.

- Hang a shallow grapevine or other basket on the door, filled with colorful gourds, ears of Indian corn, walnuts, dried pomegranates, and other gifts from Nature. Assemble your homemade cornucopia before hanging, using floral wire or hot glue; decorate with raffia ribbon.

- Using pieces of wood lattice, create a five-tiered pyramidal tree shape slightly shorter and narrower than your door. Paint it dark green, staple on some evergreen boughs, and attach the structure to the door with tacks. Decorate with small artificial pears and a partridge from a crafts store.

- Secure a large wooden or otherwise waterproof angel to the door.

Wreathed in Glory

From the days of ancient Greece, wreaths of greenery have always evoked triumph and the celebrations that go with winning a sports event. The custom of hanging a wreath at the door was passed down from the Romans, who also gave gifts of greens, called *strenae*, to

THE PASSIONATE PARASITE

Mistletoe, a parasitical plant with leathery, waxy yellow-green leaves and pearl-like berries, grows on oak, juniper, maple, apple, and poplar trees. The shrubby plant attaches itself to the host's branches and survives by sapping its mineral salts and water. In the winter when the infected trees shed their leaves, the mistletoe remains as a green mantle.

There are several species of mistletoe: American mistletoe (*Phoradendron flavescens*); European mistletoe (*Viscum album*); and dwarf mistletoe (*Arceuthobium pusillum*). The Druids of northern Europe believed that mistletoe was a sacred plant that protected one against fire and witchcraft. Among the more charming legends associated with this plant is that it was once a tree whose wood was used for Christ's crucifixion. The tree then shriveled up with shame, changing into a vine that pours down good fortune on all who pass beneath.

The Romans absorbed the mistletoe legend and the plant became a symbol of peace and goodwill. Romans, Celts, and Germanic peoples called mistletoe the Golden Bough, considering it a key to the supernatural, with powers of healing, fertility, and life over death. The Celts hung bunches of mistletoe in their homes to welcome the new year and to ward off evil. As time went by, the mistletoe became largely focused around the Christian festival of Christmas.

The belief that mistletoe brought luck may have led to the seventeenth-century British custom of the kissing ball. Another theory is that mistletoe originally served a protective, not an amorous, function. If you encountered an enemy, it was advisable to get yourself under a patch of mistletoe, where your foe was supposed to lay down his weapon and make peace with you for the rest of the day. As the custom evolved, the kissing ball was hung high over the entryway of country homes, and when a man and a woman met beneath it, it was considered fair game to steal a kiss.

The Druids regarded mistletoe as if it were a combination of penicillin, Viagra, and wolfsbane. The twigs and leaves of mistletoe (the berries are very poisonous) were used as an external medicine throughout the Middle Ages to cure falling sickness, apoplexy, and palsy. Later, preparations of mistletoe were used to treat tuberculosis, stroke, and epilepsy. Modern science has shown that it contains a host of helpful chemicals and can lower blood pressure, dilate blood vessels, and even treat arteriosclerosis.

ABOVE: **A shed gets star treatment with a garland of blue spruce, juniper, and balsam accented with holly berries and copper stars handcrafted by James Barnet.** OPPOSITE: **Spiral junipers and a large wreath, both aglow with electric lights, and a troop of candlelit lanterns forms a symmetrical arrangement.**

mark the new year. To the north, the nature-worshiping Germanic tribes also had a long tradition of crafting greens into decorations to appease evil spirits. By the sixteenth century Catholics and Protestants alike throughout Germany used wreaths adorned with candles, called Advent wreaths, to symbolize their hope in the second coming of Christ and his everlasting light. The classic wreath is a circle, a shape that represents wholeness in the cycle of the seasons and the cycle of life and can also represent a portal to another world. By hanging a wreath on your door, you are symbolically creating an opening to the world of spirit.

Although a circle always makes a beautiful wreath, it can just as easily be oval, square, lyre-, heart-, or even star- or candy-cane-shaped. Or, hang a square wreath on an angle to achieve a diamond effect. Typically, a wire, straw, grapevine, or foamcore form is used as the foundation and greens are then wired or pinned to the base. You can make your own wreaths or purchase a basic model and then make it your own. Materials range from the traditional evergreens— the many varieties of spruce, cedar, hemlock, juniper, fir, and pine—to eucalyptus, rosemary, and Russian olive, to name just a few. But wreaths can also be made from cranberries, chili peppers, horse chestnuts, magnolia leaves, sheaves of wheat, birch or manzanita switches, corn husks, or just about anything else you can find. Some greens, such as spruce and fir, can be shaped and sheared into a pyramid, a star, a fleur-de-lis, a tassel, a bell, or another shape. Check out existing shapes at a crafts store or floral-supply source or make your own forms using chicken wire or polystyrene carved into the appropriate shape.

In terms of freshness, native materials are natural winners. Why use balsam that may have traveled three thousand miles if a magnolia tree is growing in your backyard? If you live in Santa Fe, it's hard to beat a wreath of red and green chilies (the combo is called "Christmas" in local lingo). Or use fragrant pinyon, juniper, and sage, and wire on with some buffalo gourds bleached white by the sun and a few chili peppers. Likewise, if you live near California's wine country, the path of least resistance—and great beauty—might be a grapevine wreath entwined with rosemary and olive branches, plus some fool-the-eye artificial grapes.

Graced with Garlands

Almost any green suitable for a wreath can also be made into a garland, which is basically a rope of greenery held together with wire. Garlands can also be made by stringing pinecones, acorns, and pecans or other nuts in their shells, oak leaves, and many other natural items on a wire or line. Depending upon the natural form of the plant, the roping may be more or less pliant. If you want to drape a garland into small, tight forms, you'll be better off with boxwood, for example, than blue spruce or juniper. A single-weight boxwood garland will have a more delicate look and greater flexibility than several garlands woven together. But for a larger-scaled setting, you might double,

Providing a tantalizing glimpse into the festively decorated interior, a boxwood garland, studded with lights, frames a window. Inside the boxwood recurs, minus the lights.

triple, or even combine four ropes to good effect. Likewise, you can choose just one species of green or mix silver fir, incense cedar, white-edged holly, and blue spruce, for instance, for a look that is variegated in color and texture. Garlands can be casual or studied, tight or loose. Tightness, repetition, and symmetry will give the more disciplined, formal look we often associate with Colonial Williamsburg. A softer, looser, floppier, and more open look bespeaks a more casual approach better suited to a contemporary house.

Overlapping boughs of garlands should be directional. When roping goes all the way around a door, cut off a segment so that it can run in the same direction (downward) as it does on the other side. Better yet, have the two pieces meet in the center so both lengths radiate outward and down.

To further refine your garlanding technique, hide the juncture where two pieces of garland meet at, say, a corner of a doorway, with a decorative element, such as a cluster of pinecones or a big bow. To create a classic swag, or dip, in a garland, measure the distance you need to cover, then allow half again as much length; add more for a really deep swag.

In coming up with an overall plan for garlands, swags, and wreaths for your house and grounds, let the natural habit of the greens express itself, then create a rhythmic design with a variety of shapes. Also let the house tell you what it needs. If it is traditional and symmetrical, reinforce that impression with a centered swag, caught up with ribbon or wreaths in every window. If you have a pair of formal columns punctuating the entryway, acknowledge them with greens elegantly twined around them. Give a handsome railing leading up to the front door its due with swags of greenery accented with bunches of berries at each step. A fanlight over the door deserves attention, perhaps in the form of magnolia leaves arranged to radiate out, reiterating the curve of the opening. Or build on the symmetry of double doors with a pair of spiral junipers or other potted evergreens to either side covered with lights and festooned with metal ornaments. On the other hand, if your house is more contemporary you might hang an overscale wreath in front of a large window or on a solid wall, or install sheared boxwood topiaries at the entryway.

BELOW: **Garnished with jingle bells, lights, and silvery ribbons, a juniper and pine garland graces the porch of a Victorian farmhouse. Bells are hot-glued to the tails of the bow.** OPPOSITE: **Garlands, wreaths, and tartan ribbons signal a warm welcome at a Craftsman-style cottage. Even the round window in the eave gets a crown of greenery.**

Light Up the Night

The ancient Germanic people believed that a lighted candle at the window would ward off evil spirits on long winter nights. Christians later appropriated this custom to celebrate Christ's everlasting light and His spirit, and to welcome travelers seeking safe haven. Today, of course, the light is electric or battery powered, but it transmits the same messages of welcome and safety.

Strings of electric lights are capable of enormously varied atmospheric effects. Look around your property to see what plantings you might call attention to. A towering spruce is a natural candidate for illumination, but broaden your horizons beyond evergreens to look for less expected opportunities. Wrapping strings of lights around the trunk and limbs of deciduous trees such as white birches can be very dramatic. Start at the foot of your driveway with a string of

lights coiled around a signpost or the mailbox post. If you're fortunate enough to have a row of trees along either side of your driveway, artfully applied lights can call attention to your landscaping and create a dramatic sense of arrival. One of the most powerful lighting effects I have ever seen was a huge twining wisteria wrapped with thousands of lights, against a stone entry wall. Another memorable image was a patio with planters holding trees pollarded in the French style. Each tree was ablaze with light, and the planters were ringed in still more lights.

Fences and gates also offer interesting opportunities for accent lighting. On the house itself, trace the lines of an arched entryway, the windows, or even the eaves of the house with bulbs. You can use lights alone or in concert with greenery. (Battery-operated lights can come in handy if you want to light a wreath on the front door.) The trick is to plan the lighting as a whole. Exterior lighting is one of the few places where I modify my usual mantra of "More is better" to "Plenty is great—if well thought out."

Be sure to use lights specifically designed for exterior use. (The box and the tag on the string of lights will designate they are UL–listed for outdoor use, meaning they are designed to withstand the assaults of rain and snow.) My personal favorites are C-9s, long considered the traditional exterior bulb, which come in both rich opaque colors and translucent versions. Other bulbs are UL–listed for both indoor and outdoor use and include C-7s (similar to C-9s but slightly smaller), globes, floral shapes, classic mini-lights, and other designs.

Although I recommend always going for the best, this philosophy is especially important when it comes to outdoor lights. Those with weatherproof bases and fade- and peel-resistant coatings can withstand corrosive ocean air as well as conventional weather assaults. "Icicle" light sets, designed to hang from eaves, gutters, railings, and fences, have become perhaps too popular in recent years; look instead for swags of light that you can hang over porches or window frames. You can also use nets of lights (sometimes called hedge-toppers) arranged five inches apart and designed to drape over bushes and shrubs. They come with either minis-lights or C-7s. A tree-wrap design places the bulbs even closer together, at three-inch intervals. These specialty products can be a great time-saver but must be applied properly for a professional look.

OPPOSITE: **Illuminated garlands wrap around the massive framework of a log house. One wreath defines the roof pitch; another hangs from the porch railing. Kerosene lanterns on the first tier of steps give way to ice votives closer to the house. Covered with thousands of C-9 lights, a massive spruce helps light up the night.** ABOVE: **In simple contrast, an extra wreath is casually tossed over a fence post.**

TINY TREES

LIKE SO MANY of our holiday customs, the art of topiary has it roots in ancient Rome. Pliny the Younger's writings include musing on his estate in Tuscany populated with animals crafted of greenery. The Chinese and Egyptians had also discovered that they could coax plants into shapes they

Constructed of a white birch log and freeze-dried clump moss applied to a Styrofoam ball, this elegant topiary simultaneously suggests a child's drawing of a tree.

would never achieve on their own. Almost all gardening is encouraging plants to do something other than what they would do left to their own devices, but topiary is perhaps the ultimate manipulation. For all the control represented in its design philosophy, topiary is the most whimsical of the landscape arts. Just think of green giraffes, elephants, and peacocks "strolling" across a suburban lawn!

Topiary shares certain parallels to the Japanese art of bonsai and the French use of espalier (training plants to grow flat against a wall in certain patterns). Both topiary and espalier achieve shapes plants would never naturally display; and topiary for interior use and all bonsai share the concept of miniaturization, which is inherently fascinating. Topiary dovetails perfectly with the custom of bringing trees into the house at Christmastime. Living topiaries as well as topiaries composed of moss, bay leaves, lemons, cranberries, pinecones, dried rosebuds, and even Christmas ornaments are all delightful.

Alive and Well

Small living topiaries for interior use can be made in two ways. One way is to train myrtle, rosemary, box, or ivy into a shape such as a heart, a pyramid, a circle, or even a teddy bear or a watering can by using a wire, chicken wire, or mesh topiary form.

If you are handy, you can make your own frame out of bamboo stakes. There are two subgroups within this division: The frame may be stuffed with moss and soil, serving as the container and the form, or it may just provide a hollow trellis over which the plant is trained. Another method of topiary is simply to train juniper, boxwood, or an herb such as sage or rosemary into an upright lollipop, spiral, poodle pompom, or other shape, constantly pruning it into obedience. Topiaries of all sorts are available in nurseries and florists', although you will have to prune and fertilize them year-round and ensure that they are well supported as they grow. Bamboo stakes loosely tied to the stem work best.

As I am particularly attracted to symmetry, I usually arrange topiaries in pairs. Used this way, their formality is well suited to neoclassical arrangements. I also like to mass these little gems and decorate them with Christmas lights, ornaments, and ribbons, or trim them with kumquats, cranberries, or even delicate glass garlands or strands of pearls.

Gilding the Topiary

Almost any topiary can benefit from added decoration. Try some of these ideas:

• • •

Gild nuts or fruit with gold or silver leaf or metallic spray paint.

• • •

Wrap and hot-glue a string of dime-store pearls around a clay pot to dress up any topiary.

• • •

Tie raffia or ribbon around the pot; or wrap the whole pot in decorative paper or cloth and finish with a perky ribbon.

• • •

Top a pyramidal topiary with a small star and garnish with a few strands of delicate tinsel.

• • •

Tie a big bow around the stem or pole of the topiary and attach a small ornament to it.

• • •

Wire on live flowers in floral vials or freeze-dried flowers to a living topiary for an instant "graft."

Fantastical Landscapes

If living topiary is nature enhanced by the hand of man, the composed or mock topiary is an opportunity for sheer fantasy and fun. You can aim for a realistic look or a frankly faux approach. If you are making a topiary that will survive the season and be ready for next year, you will use different materials than if your work of art is meant for a one- or two-night stand.

For a long-lived topiary, look for handsome branches and materials that are dried or can dry out. Play with various-sized balls and cones (for dried materials,

Topiary Terms

There is no limit to the shapes that can be formed in topiary. Here are the most common:

· · ·

Standard One tall, straight stem with a ball on top.

· · ·

Poodle Two or three balls at intervals up the stem.

· · ·

Cone Shaped like an upside-down ice cream cone.

· · ·

Spiral Shaped like a corkscrew.

use a brown polystyrene form) to create a miniature Dr. Seuss tree or an idealized version of a Christmas tree.

In addition to using sprigs of holly, boxwood, or another green, among the natural materials you can use to create a plant of artifice are moss, artichoke leaves, dried berries, eucalyptus, lavender, yarrow, pepperberries, freeze-dried carnations, roses or other flowers, and air- or freeze-dried fruits. Velvety dried cockscomb makes a particularly dramatic topiary. For the kitchen or another casual location, adapt the old Austrian custom of the *Gewürzkranz*, or spice wreath, and use star anise, whole nutmegs,

cut-up vanilla beans, cloves, dried citrus, and cinnamon sticks to make a topiary. Several cinnamon sticks tied or glued together make the perfect trunk for the aromatic tree. Or modify pomanders made from clove-studded oranges by impaling them on a cinnamon stick and anchoring them in pots.

Short-lived topiaries, perhaps for use as a centerpiece for a dinner party, should be built upon green floral foam, which can be soaked to absorb water. Then insert vegetables, fruits, flowers, sprigs of holly, or herbs, using wire or floral pins. In addition to lemons and limes, consider such fruits as lady apples, small pears, grapes, and kumquats. A topiary of sugared and candied fruits is another party-perfect idea. Nuts are relatively long lasting and the colors of walnuts, pecans, almonds, Brazil nuts, and chestnuts provide subtle

variation. In the vegetable kingdom, radishes, artichokes, asparagus, white turnips, Brussels sprouts, and small red potatoes should provide inspiration. Be sure to mist vegetable and fresh-fruit topiaries regularly to prolong their short lives.

For pure fantasy, I love to hot-glue peppermints, gumdrops, rock sugar candy, and other sweets into sinfully sweet faux topiaries. Decorated cookies can also be used, but spray them with matte lacquer so they will not disintegrate or attract insects.

TOP, FROM LEFT TO RIGHT: **Moss-covered balls and boxes tied to simulate gifts can be kept green for weeks with regular misting. Walnut pyramids are finished with Spanish moss. "Chinese daisies" made from dyed pinecone scales will bloom indefinitely, in a topiary also made of pink pepperberries and moss.**

DECK THE HALLS

WHEN WE FILL OUR HOMES WITH GREENS, WE ARE NOT
JUST MAKING A DECORATING STATEMENT, WE ARE
RESPONDING TO SOMETHING FAR MORE ELEMENTAL.
THE ANCIENT TRADITIONS THAT CELEBRATE THE
NATURAL CYCLE OF THE SEASONS PREDATE THE BIRTH
OF CHRIST AND RESONATE WITHIN ALL OF US. AS THE
DAYS LENGTHEN AND MANY PLANTS GO INTO
HIBERNATION, ON SOME SPIRITUAL LEVEL WE ARE
POSSESSED BY AN URGE TO GO OUT AND GATHER
NATURE'S GIFTS. THE CHRISTMAS TREE MAY BE THE
PRIMARY FOCUS OF OUR DECORATIVE INSTINCTS, BUT
IT IS ONLY ONE WAY TO LITERALLY BRING SPIRIT
INTO OUR HOMES. I KNOW I LIKE TO SEE NATURE
SPROUTING EVERYWHERE IN THE HOUSE.

he hallmarks of Christmas festivities hearken back to the spiritual practices performed at ancient winter celebrations. In a backhanded way, Christianity has preserved many of these pagan customs. None is more significant than the northern European habit of bringing holly and other evergreens into the house in the dead of winter in the belief that they carried with them the sprites that lived in trees. Mankind was always trying to appease the spirit world, but tradition has it that a state of truce existed during the period now known as the twelve days of Christmas. That's why it was considered crucial that every sprig of holly and mistletoe leave the house by Twelfth Night, when the sprites were no longer to be trusted.

The ancient civilizations of Mesopotamia, Greece, Rome, and the other lands to the south also felt a spiritual kinship with plants that remained green all winter long. At the Saturnalia, the ancient Romans' festival commemorating Saturn, the god of agriculture, homes were hung with garlands. Gifts called *strenae*, often sprigs of holly, ivy, or another evergreen, were exchanged. To this day, the French call New Year's gifts *étrennes*. This festival was quickly followed by celebration of the new year, known as Kalends.

When we bring a conifer into our homes, hang kissing balls of mistletoe under our front porches, and place electrified candles in our windows, we are preserving customs whose full meanings have been blurred by time, but that resonate powerfully within our hearts. When we associate coziness with a fire in the hearth, we must have, on some atavistic level, an innate memory of lying on a wolfskin rug warmed by an open fire. Likewise, our senses are aroused by the scent of pine and balsam not only because it reminds us of our place in the natural world, but perhaps because these plants were associated with religious rites three thousand years ago.

Whatever the reasons, many of the same treatments that can turn the exterior of your house into a winter wonderland are equally suitable inside: wreaths, gar-

PREVIOUS PAGE: **Picture frames of manzanita are suspended from a ribbon that also holds a "Sugar Shack" ornament.** ABOVE: **Star, icicle, and striped glass ornaments and silver leaves and ribbons festoon a staircase.** OPPOSITE: **A Radko Neopolitan angel centered in a mixed-species wreath hangs from a ruched ribbon.**

ABOVE: **Complementing the tree reflected in the mirror, an array of living herb topiaries and a vase of cut hydrangeas in a Val Saint Lambert crystal vase is a sophisticated take on holiday décor. Topiary containers are wrapped in the same gilt tissue paper that covers gifts. A scattering of pinecones supplies the finishing touch.** OPPOSITE: **Cookies in the shape of snowflakes, candy canes, and Christmas trees team up with Radko glass ornaments and perky tricolor bows to enliven a laurel garland over a fireplace. Two painted-tin nutcracker votive holders and a Christmas tree cardholder, all by Radko, sit on the mantel.**

lands, sprays, bouquets, and other designs. Some types of greenery will not last as long in a heated environment, but you actually have far more natural options inside, such as fresh and dried flowers and herbs, where they will be safe from the destructive forces of wind, rain, and snow. And, of course, inside, you are free to use a wealth of ornaments and other decorations that would never survive outdoors.

Make the Connection

I like to see a logical link between the decorations outdoors and those within: The exterior should lay the groundwork for what you will find inside, rather like the prologue to a play or the introduction to a book. Think about relating the mood, color combinations, and even the sorts of greenery used outdoors and indoors. By all means, don't simply repeat inside what you have done outdoors; instead, provide subtle links between the two. Perhaps the wreath on your door is adorned with tiny brass hunting horns and a big

chartreuse bow. Pick up on that theme with a pair of large hunting horns anchoring a garland hung over the living-room fireplace and decorated with chartreuse streamers. Or, repeat the same color scheme for lights on an outdoor tree and the indoor tree but use the big, old-fashioned C-9 bulbs outdoors and mini-lights inside. Or, use star-shaped lightbulbs on shrubs and hang a constellation of glass star ornaments inside the window overlooking them. You'll find it is fun to see if your visitors pick up on such connections.

It's usually a good idea to maintain the same general style from outdoors to indoors as well. It's jarring to go from Colonial Williamsburg–elegant to primitive country inside, or from bold contemporary outside to hidebound traditional inside. Pick one approach and stick with it, allowing plenty of room for variety and surprise from room to room. Color is a tried-and-true way to connect and distinguish. For example, you might decide on a classic red–green color scheme for the living room, then vary it to green and pink in the dining room, green and gold in the kitchen, red and gold in the den, and gold and white in the entry. Such an approach is not unlike picking a family of paint colors to link adjoining rooms. The result is interesting, rather than disconcerting, as it would be if the colors seemed unrelated to those in adjacent spaces.

OPPOSITE: **Elegant French wired ribbon is carefully shaped to grace a circle of boxwood along with "Purple Plum" ornaments and "sugared" faux berries. A delicate glass garland traces the folds of a damask valance.** ABOVE: **With the stars and stripes blowing proudly outside, a natural wreath trimmed with a few artificial frosted sprigs and blue, white, and silver ribbons hangs beneath a constellation of beaded glass stars suspended from fishing line.** TOP RIGHT: **A fantasy of artificial greens: Radko fruit, flower, and globe ornaments (including "Rosy Love Birds") and silk flowers and leaves hangs between a pair of leaded-glass French doors. A two-piece glass tassel ornament hangs from the bow.** RIGHT: **Real clementines and walnuts wired to a fresh wreath provide a haven for a Santa holding a tiny feather tree and a toy lamb.** NEXT PAGE: **In the living room of the governor of Connecticut's house, a robust garland composed of magnolia leaves and artificial greens is caught up with elaborate bows at the corners and a Radko Neapolitan angel in the center. Magnolia leaves wreathe the mirror.**

Another approach is simply to follow the color scheme already established in a room. At the official residence of the governor of Connecticut we followed the interior designer's lead. In the dining room, where the walls wore a wonderful rose damask, we decided to use glass ornaments depicting fruit primarily in pink and red and festooned with pink French wired ribbon. Pink peonies and red roses completed the lush look. In the living room, where walls were painted sky blue, we used blue and gold ribbons, glass ornaments, and lush greenery. In the study, which is paneled in richly stained wood, we played up the men's-club look with autumnal colors, pinecone- and acorn-shaped glass ornaments, and golden leaves. The colors in each room were very different, but the connective tissue was the mood and the use of greenery, ribbon, and glass ornaments.

There's no need to confine yourself to a strict color scheme. If you are attracted to a multitude of colors, indulge yourself much as the Victorians did with their exuberant approach to Christmas. What you might not dare in terms of interior décor, you are free to do with Christmas decorations.

If you have a large collection of ornaments, take a tip from collector Fred Cannon (whose home was photographed for this book) and organize your decorating scheme around different types. One room in his Brooklyn row house shows off contemporary handmade ornaments; another, his collection of vintage American patriotic trinkets (oddly enough, most made in Germany before World War II); another, cardboard Dresdens. Or you may want to concentrate on, say, a food motif in one room, mixing up a concoction of sugarplums, gingerbread cookies, candy canes, and other delicacies, both real and in the form of fanciful ornaments. Other possible themes include Santa Claus, *The Nutcracker*, teddy bears, antique toys, angels, or sea creatures and other things associated with the ocean.

Inspired by Architecture

Just as you should take your lead from the exterior architecture, look to interior features such as doorways, bay windows, mantelpieces, niches, and staircases when deciding what and how to decorate for the holidays. (Fireplaces are discussed in "At the Hearth," beginning on page 116.) Treat your furniture as architecture. A gracefully arched highboy, a curvy-topped armoire, or a formal breakfront all lend

BELOW: **Made by Susan Shroyer from a pattern published more than a century ago in** *Godey's Lady's Book,* **Santa has arms and legs made from Norway pinecones.** OPPOSITE: **A Della Robbia treatment of fruits and nuts enhances a Federal-style mirror. Kathy Patterson, who made this Santa, had the basket woven especially in France. The doll behind it and the grape-shaped** *Kugel* **are antique.**

themselves to the kind of decorative treatments appropriate to windows and doorways. Although the style of your house and décor will most likely be a source of inspiration, that is not to say that you cannot deliberately counter it if you do so with confidence. We've all seen wonderful examples of traditional homes superbly decorated with contemporary furnishings, and there's no reason not to do the same with Christmas treatments. It's more important to have fun and do what your heart tells you than to feel you have to follow rules. After all, if your great experiment fizzles a bit, do it differently next year.

In many ways, holiday decorating frees you from the usual design strictures.

For example, you can accentuate the sweeping lines of a curving staircase with fabulous garlands. But Christmas décor is equal-opportunity design: You can just as easily lend drama to a featureless staircase. As you survey your house looking for inspiration, think also about what uninteresting or even problematic feature might improve significantly with the addition of decoration. The opening between your living room and dining room may be defined with merely a skimpy three-inch stock molding. Here's your chance to make the transition far more powerful by covering that anorexic trim with plump evergreen roping caught with golden tassels. No one but you need know what lies beneath your dramatic treatment. In that respect, Christmas decorating is more like stage design than interior design: It is inherently dramatic, full of artifice, and deliberately transitory.

In mining decorative opportunities, look beyond the four walls. The ceiling offers light fixtures begging for decoration. A high ceiling can look positively magical with garlands of greens swagged from one corner of the room to another, perhaps caught up in the center with a chandelier or over the Christmas tree. Furniture can step beyond its utilitarian role for the holidays as well. Sideboards, secretaries, bookcases, even beds call out for attention. A classic treatment for large pieces of furniture is to drape white pine or other evergreens over the top with short jabots hanging at the side. Fan magnolia leaves around the top of a mirror or tuck sprigs of holly over a collection of pictures for a festive note. Garlands are wonderfully egalitarian decorations, as at home encircling a banister and newel post as they are tracing the arch of a Palladian window.

Let's take a virtual tour of a typical house or apartment to get a sense of the whole holiday decorating process.

Doorway to Decoration

Your first impression once inside is usually of one of the smallest spaces in the house: the front hall or foyer. Turn that limitation into an advantage with a dramatic statement that immediately declares "Merry Christmas" and hints at the wonders that lie beyond. Perhaps it is a small tabletop tree decorated to the nines. Perhaps it is a pair of wonderful topiaries, a grove of potted poinsettia plants, or

OPPOSITE: **The front hall of Lyndhurst, the Gothic-style house built in 1838 and now a National Trust property, demands the full Radko treatment of garlands bedecked with ribbons and hundreds of glass ornaments. "Royal Star" finials serve as drops at the garland ends. Topiaries made of hot-glued ornaments and bows are banked with potted poinsettias. A "Razzmatazz" kissing ball hangs from the lantern.** ABOVE: **Pheasant feathers, ribbons, and C-7 lights accent a fireplace adorned with "Kaleidoscope Cone," "Winter Acorn," and "Frosted Oak" ornaments.**

an enchanted garden of Christmas blooms. Or maybe it is an antique Santa Claus welcoming both visitors and the season. Perhaps it is the staircase encircled with an incredibly intricate garland made of ornaments and glass garlands.

Whatever you decide on, the impact should be immediate. This is also your opportunity to engage as many of your guests' senses as possible with scented

A pair of framed die-cut chromolithograph "scraps" hangs over a sink alcove in the bedroom of a Victorian row house. Printed in Germany in the 19th century, the images depict Christmas subjects. A cranberry-glass light fixture and a bouquet of red tulips enhance the holiday spirit.

flowers, evergreens, potpourri, and bells that jingle when the door opens or a Christmas-carol CD rigged up to the doorbell. Continue with the concept of Christmas decorating being like stage design and decorate your foyer to make each arrival an event worthy of a curtain call.

Don't forget to turn around and look back at the front door. When your guests leave, you want the final impression to be another lasting one. Hang a wreath at the door and trace the molding with a garland on the inside as well as the outside. If there isn't one outside, be sure to hang a kissing ball. (Buy a wire form, then wind ivy or boxwood around the armature and suspend a sprig of mistletoe.) Punctuate a pair of sidelights with topiaries, Norway pines, or another symmetrical treatment. The truth is, you will see far more of the inside of the door than the outside, so do it up right. Likewise, transitions from one area to another, whether inside to outside or from one room to another, all beg for acknowledgment.

Impressive Openings

The classic treatment of accentuating doors and windows with garlands and swags is as appealing indoors as it is outside. Likewise, wreaths are equally at home inside, hung on windows or doors, over the fireplace, accenting beams, or wherever a touch of greenery is needed.

Before hanging anything, look at how your doors and windows open. Double-hung sashes usually require no special treatment, but you need to know how casement windows and French doors swing. If they open out, you can hang a swag in front of them (in the case of doors, this works only if they are not used very often—perhaps a patio door that is rarely used in cold weather). If the door is in constant use, or the doors or windows open in, make sure that your arrange-

THE HOLLY AND THE IVY

IVY was considered sacred to the Greek god Dionysus, known in ancient Rome as Bacchus, and has long been associated with alcohol consumption and bawdy behavior. But the plant later gained a more respectable image, its evergreen nature making it a symbol for eternity. Victorious athletes in Sparta were crowned with a wreath of ivy. The plant's split personality continued into the Middle Ages, where it was either cultivated to decorate churches or considered a wanton plant. By the eighteenth century ivy reached the apex of its popularity, both for landscaping purposes (think of Ivy League–college buildings) and as a houseplant favored for training into living topiaries. There are a dozen types of ivy, with numerous variations of color, leaf shape, and size. Ivy's evergreen leaves and trailing habit make it an ideal plant for both interior and exterior holiday décor.

HOLLY, ivy's traditional partner, makes a strange bedfellow. Unlike ivy, which is a vine, holly is a shrub or a tree, but both have played a large role in legend and lore. Holly, too, is a favorite of topiary artists. The Druids held holly sacred, believing the sun never deserted it. Bringing holly inside in the dead of winter allowed them to decorate their homes while providing protection for woodland sprits. Other ancient cultures imbued holly with the symbolic virtues of foresight and goodwill. Holly has often been associated with the male, representing the steadfast and the holy and the clinging ivy symbolic of maidenly love and friendship.

As with so many pagan customs, the early Christians co-opted the symbolic value of holly, suggesting that its name was a corruption of the word "holy" and that Christ's crown of thorns was made of holly. The bloodred berries only strengthened the association and holly has long been associated with Christmas celebrations. Among the many customs associated with holly is one that beehives should be adorned with a sprig of holly in order to wish the bees a merry Christmas.

The stereotypical holly depicted on endless Christmas cards and wrapping paper is American holly (*Ilex opaca*). Chinese holly (*I. cornuta* 'Burfordii') offers much larger bunches of berries. Yaupon holly (*I. vomitoria*) has porcelain-white berries and makes a delightful partner to cut flowers. Although most hollies are notable for their showy green leaves, some have cream-colored edges or are variegated throughout. Deciduous hollies lose their leaves in winter, making the brilliant red or orange berries of possumhaw holly (*I. decidua*) and winterberry (*I. verticillata*) all the more dramatic. Most florists carry a variety of hollies during the holidays. Out of water, holly dries out quickly. But it will last two to three weeks if you recut the stems and change the water regularly.

TOP: **Tendrils of ivy twist around a topiary made with fresh pears. "Grandmother's Garden" glass globes hang from the window frame.** ABOVE: **Sprigs of holly accent frame late-eighteenth- and nineteenth-century silhouettes.**

LEFT: **A fresh laurel garland, accented with a
wreath of rosemary, gar-
nishes a breakfast room
window. On the antique
table, a bouquet of red
cabbage, cauliflower,
peppers, other vegeta-
bles, and fresh herbs
extends the culinary
theme. Hollowed-out
artichokes serve as
votive candleholders.**
BELOW: **A pot ringed with
faux pearls supports a
mossy angel topiary.
Scented gel candles emit
a mysterious glow.**

ment is self-contained so it moves with either door or window. To avoid the naked look inside when a wreath is hung on a window outdoors, double up with another one of the same size on the inside.

The simplest way to accent a doorway or a window without an elaborate drapery or other window treatment is to attach a spray of greenery above it, graced with a ribbon and a few ornaments. For a bolder look, swag a length of garland from one corner of the door or window to another, acknowledging the corners with bows, a bunch of pinecones mixed with ornaments, or another punctuation point. A full treatment would add a pair of garlands that fall from the corners midway down the molding or to the floor. These side pieces correspond to the jabots in a swag-and-jabot window treatment. For ease in handling, you'll want to make the garland and its jabot segments in three pieces, one for each side and one for the center. Hide the juncture at each corner with extra pieces of greenery, bows, or other design component. And keep the direction of the greenery in mind when installing the garland so that it is consistent on either side.

Classic as they are, swags and jabots offer limitless opportunities for creativity. For example, double or triple a purchased garland to augment the degree of lushness. Roping that looks skimpy by itself can become positively plump when entwined with a twin. Or double the swag, but use single ropes for the jabots.

A garland need not be composed of only one kind of greenery: Weave together contrasting greens, such as Scotch pine, juniper, false cypress (*Chamaecyparis*), which have dark green, blue-green, and chartreuse foliage, respectively. Sprigs of variegated holly would add yet another color note. By itself, green holly can appear too dense and uniform. It takes well to needled plants such as white pine, cypress, cedar, and juniper. Consider texture and sheen as well as color when mixing evergreen species. Finally, tuck in branches of aromatic plants such as eucalyptus, rosemary, thyme, and bay leaves, plus some berries for

TOOLS OF THE TRADE

A few gadgets and accessories will make the job of creating garlands and other decorations easier.

- Gardening gloves come in handy when working with holly, rose hips, and other thorny boughs or sharp-needled evergreens such as spruce.
- A glue gun and glue sticks can be used for everything from applying seedpods to wreaths to attaching ornament caps securely.
- Floral foam absorbs water, extending the life of natural arrangements.
- Floral wire (both plain and cloth-coated) strengthens delicate stems and, with a few twists, attaches berries, pinecones, and just about anything else. The wire comes in cut lengths and on spools and coils.
- Floral netting can form the base of a wreath or garland.
- Floral picks are slivers of wood like large toothpicks with a thin wire attached to one end. Insert them into a polystyrene or straw base, and then tie on some berries, fruit, or a ribbon.
- Pins, also called greening pins, are the floral equivalent of bobby pins or hairpins. Another kind is shaped like a T. They attach moss to a straw or polystyrene base and can also hold unruly greenery and flowers in place.
- Floral clay, or sticky clay, secures arrangements and can corral one plant close to another.
- Florist's vials, small stoppered glass or plastic containers, extend the life of fresh-cut plants.

color. (See "Winter Wonderland," on page 48, for more on greens and berries.)
Garlands and wreaths can also be a twig or polystyrene frame to which you
attach moss and then sprigs of greenery and other decorations.

Even windows with formal draperies can dress up for the holidays, much as a
woman dons jewelry to jazz up a basic dress for a night on the town. Reiterate
the lines of the draperies with swagged glass garlands or use one as a tieback.
To accent drapery tiebacks, attach one or more ornaments as "earrings" tied
with a pretty ribbon.

For a dramatic and magical look that is particularly suited to contemporary

interiors, try hanging a "curtain" of light, using numerous strings of miniature lights hung from the top of the window to the floor.

Stairway to Heaven

The custom of decorating the staircase is a particularly charming one, because it incorporates the sense of holiday anticipation that dwells in any house with children. The image of the little darlings peeking over the banister and then traipsing downstairs in pajamas and bathrobes to see what Santa has brought is a poignant icon in our culture. The staircase also symbolizes the distinction between the public and private parts of the house. When it is an architectural focal point, seen the moment you enter the house, there's all the more reason to decorate it appropriately.

My favorite stairwell approach is to start with a base of greenery, then build upon it for a tour de force of glass ornaments, glass garlands, and ribbons, all heightened with twinkling lights. Let the lines of the staircase guide you as you decide how frequent and deep to make the garland dip into swags. A curving wrought-iron banister will demand a different approach from a straightforward staircase with wooden banisters. Whatever the shape, ornaments should be attached on the outside so that you don't brush against them as you climb or descend. At the base, where the steps often widen, you can usually find space to add some ornamentation to the inside. Typically, the base is the most heavily ornamented area, but if you are fortunate enough to have a landing, you have another opportunity for a special treatment.

In a contemporary setting, you might want to try tightly wrapping the balustrades with lights and looping only the handrail with greens for a restrained but dramatic approach. In a rustic house, we often strategically place baskets filled with greens and ornaments every few feet along a garlanded banister. If space allows, try placing a small decorated tree, topiary, or floor vase filled with greenery

FRESHNESS COUNTS

Florist Marlo Phillips arranged white Norwegian spruce, pink pepperberries, brown velvet protea, rose hips, echinacea, and raspberry sunflowers in a majolica urn (above). To keep greens fresh, she advises the following:

- Buy early in the season before greens have had a chance to dry out.
- Cut and place purchased greens in water for a day before using.
- Before arranging, spritz or dip greens into a cold bath to remove dust.
- Spritz greens daily.
- Use floral foam wreaths and swags and shape to fit in a waterproof container, then water regularly. (This trick can also prolong the life of an outdoor arrangement on, say, a lamppost.)
- Turn the heat down as low as is comfortable, especially at night, and use a humidifier.

OPPOSITE: **A cottage staircase is draped with juniper, spruce, and Japanese lanterns. Baskets hold dried pomegranates, oranges, artichokes, gourds, and sticks of cinnamon. A tramp art picture frame joins the rustic arrangement.**

ABOVE: Patchwork quilts and hooked and woven rugs take on Christmas airs in a child's bedroom. Vintage cards and candy canes on each red plaid flannel pillowcase hint at bigger treats to come. Other holiday touches: a boxwood heart wreath hanging at the window, cookies and milk set out between the beds, and a bow embellishing the door-knob. LEFT: The appliqué designs in the two pillows made in Hungary were cut from wool felt. OPPOSITE: In another bedroom, ivy twines over a painted metal footboard and gifts decorated with ivy and holly atop an antique chest.

at the base of a curving staircase. It will anchor the arrangement and provide interest as you descend the steps. If you have pictures hanging on the stairwell wall, give them each a little Yule boost by topping each with a sprig of holly or spruce. As always, don't forget your sense of humor. A friend has a marvelous collection of pencil studies of classical sculpture that march up his tall stairwell. During the holidays, he attaches a tiny crocheted green and red wreath to one hand of each figure depicted in a drawing. I smile every time I climb his staircase.

Opportunities Abound

Every room in the house deserves a little Christmas cheer. Why not put a pine-scented votive in the powder room and tie your guest towels with a red ribbon, tucking in a fir sprig? Children's bedrooms are particularly deserving of decoration. If they are old enough, encourage your kids to come up with their own themes. As a youngster, I loved to decorate a silvery artificial tree discarded by the family with creations I'd made at school. Whether decorated with gingerbread cookies, teddy bears, paper or popcorn garlands, or even plastic dinosaurs, a tree created by a child has its own special poignancy. Perhaps you can borrow your daughter's dollhouse to decorate for Christmas. And convince your son to loan out his train set to chug around the tree. Toys are always fitting decorations for this holiday that celebrates the joy and innocence of children the world over.

For a romantic touch in the master bedroom, why not put mistletoe to good use with a kissing ball hung over the bed? Four-poster beds lend themselves to wearing garlands of ivy and other trailing greens. Even a pretty wreath on the headboard will infuse the room with holiday spirit. Place a few potted junipers festooned with ribbons at the foot of the bed. Or fill a graceful silver pitcher with pink roses and holly leaves. Just because this is personal space is no reason not to display some of your favorite decorations.

Light fixtures often call out for adornment. A chandelier hanging in the front hall or over a dining table is a natural for a Christmas outfit of greens and some dangling ornaments or glass garlands. For a natural look, entwine a brass or wrought-iron chandelier with ivy or bittersweet, perhaps mixed with garlands of cranberries and kumquats or lady apples. A simple hanging fixture can often provide the framework for an Advent wreath, which traditionally holds three white candles and one red one. Trim wall sconces with a sprig of greenery and an ornament tied in a bow.

Take another look at your houseplants. Your little Norway pine may be just pining for some tiny ornaments and a few pretty bows on the tips of its delicate branches. Bring in a handsome tree branch from outdoors, perhaps witch hazel or crab apple, to force it into flower. Even a bare tree branch with an elegant shape can become a venue for decoration (just be sure to secure it in a weighted pot before hanging ornaments from it). Another charming idea is to make a miniature landscape of moss, twigs, stones, and votive candles. For more ideas, see "The Art of Display," on page 136.)

Multiple Materials

Many of the same materials suitable for outdoor use —vines, greenery, and other weatherproof natural and artificial materials—work equally well inside, but here, unfettered by the vagaries of weather, why not push the possibilities even further? For instance, the basis for an indoor garland might be dried pinky-green hydrangeas, or an indoor wreath can be crafted of brilliant scarlet dried cockscomb, neither of which would fare well outside. Dried rosebuds, baby's breath, yarrow, heather, statice, and lavender last for several years. Dried plants such as wheat, sedges, Spanish moss, silver dollars (also called Memory), and Japanese lanterns, which are too delicate for outdoor use, can tuck into vines of bittersweet and rose hips. Fresh-cut flowers such as roses, carnations, and orchids are suitable only indoors. Placed in small glass or plastic vials sold at florists' and crafts-supply stores, fresh blooms could last up to a week as a delightful component of an evergreen arrangement. Such treatment will also extend the life of ivy, herbs, and other fresh greens. Freeze-dried blooms, veggies, and fruit will last for several years if handled properly (see "Realer Than Real" on page 101). And, of course, glass ornaments and glass garlands make even

ABOVE: **Above a kitchen hearth a harvest of goodies—dried Japanese lanterns, Indian corn, gourds, pumpkins, squash, and limes— signal the bountifulness of the season.** OPPOSITE: **A stairwell garland mixes fresh ivy and plumosa and leatherleaf ferns with freeze-dried pansies, liatris, black-berries, larkspur, misty, rice flower, lepto, and heather.**

REALER THAN REAL

Beautiful as fresh flowers, fruits, and veggies are, they have an annoying habit of
dying or going bad. If only the real thing will do, you have several longer-lasting options:

GLYCERIN-PRESERVED GREENS have been dehydrated
and the water replaced with glycerin for a look that is
much more live-looking than air-dried plants. The scent
is also preserved. Cedar, boxwood, pepperberries,
heather, salal, several varieties of eucalyptus, caspia,
bay leaves on the bough, bracken and other ferns, and
lemon, magnolia, and camellia leaves are all available in
this form.

FREEZE-DRYING achieves the most realistic effects. In
the case of flowers, the open blooms are sprayed with a
chemical that sets the colors. The temperature is then
dropped to −30 degrees Fahrenheit. After the flowers
are frozen solid, the air is pumped out of the chamber to
create a vacuum. The temperature is then gradually
raised. Finally, the dry flowers are dipped in a polymer
to prevent them from reabsorbing moisture. Rosebuds,
roses in full bloom in numerous
colors and sizes, gardenias,
carnations, ranunculus, calla
lilies, dogwood flowers,
peonies, Queen Anne's lace,
and sunflowers are just some
of the posies you can find. The
same process can be applied
to fruits, including lemons,
limes, oranges, crab apples,
apples, kiwi, blackberries,
strawberries, and pomegranates. Some come in whole and
sliced versions. Artichokes,
asparagus, Brussels sprouts,
eggplants, gourds, pumpkins,
and potatoes represent the
vegetable world. The produce
not only look just picked, they

are much lighter than fresh versions and easier to attach
to wreaths, garlands, even the tree. The only caveat
with freeze-dried plants is that they will deteriorate in
high humidity. Also, they may need to be treated to keep
them from attracting moths and other pests.

FOR FREEZE-DRIED BOTANICALS:
WILSON EVERGREENS (*www.wilsonevergreens.com*)
makes preserved autumn-color oak leaf wreaths in two-
and three-foot diameters and ten-foot garlands. Or you
can order a wreath of oak leaves mixed with birch
branches.

FLYBOY NATURALS (800-465-5125; *www.flyboynatu-
rals.com*) sells such freeze-dried flowers as larkspur,
dogwood, camellias, and gardenias as well as roses from
around the world. Freeze-dried fruits include lemons,
oranges, limes, crab apples,
apples, pomegranates, black-
berries, and strawberries.
Vegetables include artichokes,
eggplants, gourds, and
pumpkins.

LILAC ROSE (903-438-1716;
www.lilacrose.com) is another
supplier of freeze-dried flowers. Look for roses, calla lilies,
carnations, gardenias, peonies,
and Queen Anne's lace, among
other blooms. Preserved greenery includes boxwood, lemon
magnolia, salal, and eucalyptus
leaves, plus bay leaves on their
branches. Bracken ferns are
also available.

the simplest arrangement of greens take on indoor manners.

Another source of inspiration is as close as your spice shelf. Cinnamon sticks are a classic Christmas craft item; in fact, you're better off buying them in a crafts store than a supermarket. Star anise, dried vanilla beans, whole nutmegs, and cloves can also be used. Aromatic spice wreaths called *Gewürzkranze* have been made in Austria for generations.

Just as there are proponents of fresh-cut Christmas trees versus fans of quality artificial trees, there is an ongoing debate about the use of artificial greenery and other nature-inspired decorations. My position is wholeheartedly middle-of-the-road. I love the aroma and the look of fresh-cut greens, but the reality is that it is hard to keep them looking terrific for more than a couple of weeks. Artificial greens have no such problems but you must be discriminating in which ones you use. There are lush look-alikes you have to feel and sniff to tell for sure they aren't the genuine article, and then there are the all-too-common bargain-basement knockoffs. If it doesn't look real, pass it by. (For more on artificial greenery, see "Almost Green" on page 106.)

The real trick is to mix real and artificial greens and other natural (or almost natural) elements. Interestingly, if most of an arrangement is made from living plants, your eye and brain usually read the whole arrangement as natural. With this in mind, we often use an artificial garland as a base, then interweave living greenery. Real greenery can be accented with artificial berries, which can look startlingly real without the nuisance of drying out and dropping to the floor. Imitations of ivy and other vines are often extremely convincing and quality silk flowers can fool almost anyone. If a plant dries well—eucalyptus, for example—my instinct is to select it over an artificial version. On the other hand, some outright fantasies, such as gold and silver leaves, are just fine. If you put aside any prejudices about everything having to be natural, you can mix fresh-cut, dried, and artificial plants to fabulous effect. Remember, it is a look you are going for, not a prize for 100 percent authenticity. Christmas decorating is all

ABOVE: **Pecans in their shells are wired into a boxwood garland hanging in front of outward-opening French doors.** OPPOSITE: **A garland of bay leaves, lavender, rosemary, thyme, sage, and juniper berries dresses up an antique French rack in the corner of a kitchen. Boughs of rosemary and bunches of lavender line the shelves. A batch of Christmas cookies is in the making at the antique gateleg table.**

LEFT: Glass balls nestle
in a nursery flat and
pots of lush wheat
grass. On the table
behind the sofa, silvery
glass "Snowmagic" gar-
lands and "Constella-
tion" beaded ornaments
bedeck branches of crab
apple in a rusticated
urn. Glass hurricanes
filled with more pastel
glass globes hold can-
dles. BELOW: In the
same room, a spray of
bleached wheat caught
in an organdy bow and
topiary balls made of
tiny pinecones comprise
another vignette.

about fantasy, and you might as well enter into the spirit wholeheartedly!

With this attitude in mind, a visit to a crafts-supply store can be a mind-opening experience. Here you will find basic wreaths made of dried boxwood or sprays of eucalyptus that you can personalize, as well as wreath forms of straw, excelsior, wire, or polystyrene in a variety of sizes and shapes such as stars, hearts, fans, and demilune door toppers. Other wreaths made of bent willow, honeysuckle, huckleberry twigs, and birch twigs call out for ornamentation. Particularly effective in their trompe l'oeil forms are ferns, juniper branches, bunches of grapes, and strings of cranberries and lady apples. Evergreen boughs in unnatural but wonderfully effective shades of gold, silver, and white—in moderation—could tuck beautifully into a live wreath or garland.

You're likely to find a good variety of dried plants, many from faraway lands. In addition to the attractive but expected boxwood, statice, lavender, wheat, and eucalyptus, look for delicate bloom-broom, glossy lemon leaves, thistlelike echinopis, the green-and-brown-striped pods of Nigella, and robust artichokes. Rods of curly willow, cinnamon sticks bigger than any you'll see in the spice aisle, and exotic lotus pods all have their own charm. You'll also find dried poppy heads, pomegranates, nuts, and seedpods as well as dried slices of apples, oranges, lemons, and quince.

The artificial-flower department requires a more vigilant eye. The selection is enormous but the quality and verisimilitude vary greatly. If you are willing to spend the money, you are likely to find better quality at a specialty store or florist. However, check out other departments before you leave the crafts store. The wedding section may have a nice selection of white, gold, and silver flowers—some accented with pearls—and leaves for millinery use. And shops that sell millinery supplies offer wonderful fake flowers and fruits perfect for Christmas décor.

Don't overlook fresh produce. Pomegranates, red and green apples, lemons, limes, and kumquats beckon from the grocery. Go beyond the expected and consider using pineapple (the traditional symbol of welcome), artichokes (hollowed out, they make wonderful holders for votive candles), winter squash, and other fruits and vegetables. If you plan on keeping your decorations up for weeks, use dried, freeze-dried, or artificial fruits and veggies instead of fresh ones.

ALMOST GREEN

Quality artificial greenery, like artificial Christmas trees, has become increasingly realistic in recent years, but you do have to pay for it. Avoid loss-leader garlands sold for $1.99 and expect to pay $15 or so for a nine-foot rope. To enhance their verisimilitude, mix different "species." In addition to lasting virtually forever and shedding nary a needle, man-made greenery is lighter and can support more lights than true greens. Always fluff up the needles, then straighten them out so they look realistic. Also double up on garlands for a dense look. Use green plastic ties that lock together like handcuffs to attach to banisters. A few small nails in the molding (or fishing line attached to the nail) will hold a garland in place over a window or door.

ABOVE: A cheerful front hall celebrates the holiday season even as it hints of spring. The deep box bay is upholstered with club moss (laid on plastic sheeting) and topped with lush arrangements of white amaryllis, tulips, and narcissus in rusted urns. A double garland of boxwood is caught up with raffia bows at the corners; a single garland cascades to the floor. RIGHT: Pink and pale green pair up for an evocative tableau consisting of a collection of copper-luster cups and pitchers plus a bouquet of eucalyptus pods, hydrangea, and pepperberries, a bowl of pomegranates, and a bunch of green dates. Vintage Christmas cards tuck into a metal flower-arranging frog. A beeswax pillar adds to the romantic mood.

For the finishing touch, ribbon comes in a myriad of colors, styles, and sizes. You should find a good variety in any crafts or notions store. A whole book could be written about ribbons, but those appropriate for holiday decoration fall into a few categories. A Radko signature look is French wired ribbon, often used in three contrasting or complementary colors. Velvet ribbon is wonderfully lush; satin (look for double-faced satin so there is no "wrong" side when you tie a bow) has a wonderfully fluid "hand." Moiré ribbon has a shimmery effect and a rather stiff hand, as does taffeta. Organza is as gossamer as a dragonfly's wing. Incidentally, many beautiful ribbons are made of rayon as well as silk. Ribbons can be tied into classic bows, triple cloverleaves, or rosettes, or allowed to stream free. Cording and raffia, which comes in various widths, add to the fun.

Consider these other ideas for making garlands and wreaths even more interesting and personal:

- Tuck in or wire on pinecones, nuts, leaves, dried mushrooms, feathers, or moss. Also use fruits and berries, whether natural or good copies.

- In the kitchen, use small whisks, measuring spoons, wooden spoons, cinnamon sticks, star anise, citrus fruit pomanders, and other food-inspired ornaments.
- Give culinary herbs another purpose with a wreath or swag made of rosemary, sage, and other fragrant woody herbs. Garnish with chili peppers, heads of garlic, small gourds, and freeze-dried or artificial veggies.
- Strategically place a good-size figure of Santa, an angel, a doll, a dove or other bird, or a teddy bear in the center or to the side of a wreath.
- Attach decorated cookies, tiny boxes wrapped to look like gifts, tiny felt or fabric stockings, or images cut from last year's Christmas cards.
- Illuminate with small Christmas lights in unusual color combinations. Or use light covers that depict Santa, tiny Christmas trees, or other subjects.
- Gild some of the leaves of broad-leaf plants such as olive, bay, and magnolia in gold, silver, or copper to heighten the contrast with their own natural color. You can also gild pinecones and/or nuts and bunch them in clusters with wire alongside those wearing their own more subdued colors.

TOP CENTER: **Eucalyptus leaves and berries filled in with pepperberries arranged on the mantel and around the wall sconces repeat the colors of the striped fabric that upholsters the walls.** ABOVE: **Radko "Pomegranate," "Apple a Day," "Golden Pear," "Razzle Berry," and "Sugar Pear" glass ornaments, artificial berries, and wired French ribbon playfully enhance a classic breakfront.**

SAY IT WITH FLOWERS

ALONG WITH HOLLY and misletoe, a plant intimately connected with Christmas is the poinsettia *(Euphorbia pulcherrima)*, a native of Mexico whose Latin name means "very beautiful." In December, legions of these plants herald the season in florists' shops, nurseries, and even supermarkets, making them the most popular potted plant in the United States. (Ironically, what we call flowers are actually bracts surrounding insignificant yellow flowers.)

Another flower associated with the holiday, Star-of-Bethlehem *(Ornithogalum arabicum)*, is a cluster of small green bells that open to form white, star-shaped flowers. The cup-shaped blooms of hellebores *(Hellebores foetidus)* are also known as Christmas roses and the Christmas cactus is so named because it blooms in December. Other flowers commonly associated with Christmas include amaryllis, paper-white narcissus, and cyclamen. These and other cut flowers and flowering houseplants add another layer of festivity—and scent—to the house.

Elsewhere in this book, flowers are discussed as materials for garlands and wreaths and even as decorations on Christmas trees, but blossoms obviously also deserve pride of place in bouquets. One could spend a lifetime studying and perfecting all the forms of flower arranging, but for simplicity's sake, we will look at three basic approaches. One technique is to mass one vari-

OPPOSITE: **Florist Marlo Phillips mixed Mister Lincoln hybrid tea roses and rose hips with "Pomegranate," "Ruby Red," and Melon Slice" ornaments for a stunning centerpiece.** ABOVE: **A vase of candy-cane amaryllis in a Val Saint Lambert crystal vase and additional blooms in bowls nestle in an island of clump moss.**

The Force Be with You

Forcing bulbs into bloom for Christmas display is relatively easy as long as you get your act together in time.

• • •

Paper-white narcissus require only about two weeks in a cool, dark location before being brought into a lighted, heated room. The bulbs can be grown in water and anchored with pebbles or gravel in a shallow bowl.

• • •

Precooled hyacinths require six to eight weeks to grow. Specially designed hyacinth glasses suspend the bulbs just above the water; or just use a glass or a teacup. After the bulbs display a topknot of foliage, move them to successively brighter locations.

• • •

Amaryllis bulbs are grown in soil in a container about twice as deep as the bulb itself. Top with sheet or clump moss, wheatgrass, or Spanish moss for a finished look. Amaryllis also take about six to eight weeks to develop blooms. Be sure to rotate plants to encourage straight stems, and keep in a cool location.
Amaryllis bulbs can be reused; other forced bulbs are usually thrown out, but it doesn't hurt to try planting them in the garden come spring. Feel free to cut forced bulbs for use in bouquets.

ety for impact. Another is to mix several types of flowers within a color family; for example, combining several colors and shapes of red tulips, roses, ranunculus, and salvia. Finally, you can blend several shades and shapes in anything from a nosegay to a massive arrangement evocative of seventeenth-century Dutch paintings. Cut-flower arrangements benefit from the addition of greens, herbs, and twigs such as curly willow, seedpods, and other plant parts. The resulting myriad of looks can range from highly stylized and formal displays to relaxed and natural groupings. In addition to all the evergreens and berried branches cited on pages 53 and 58, feel free to mix in branches of pussy willow or curly willow, red dogwood (*Cornus alba*), and canes of bamboo. Or, add red and orange ornamental peppers (*Capsicum frutescens*), decorative kale (*Brassica*), rosemary, and other herbs and vegetables to achieve a look of abundance.

Seasonal Colors

Combinations of red, cream, and green are particularly effective at Christmastime, perhaps incorporating red and cream roses, hellebores, and fluffy scarlet plume (*Euphorbia fulgens*). When you think about red, open your mind also to the wonderful hues ranging from pale pink to salmon and coral, to magenta and burgundy. Tulips (*Tulipa*), amaryllis (*Hippeastrum*), and roses (*Rosa*) immediately spring to mind, but look also for brilliantly hued Gerber daisies (*Gerbera*), *Dendrobium* and *Cymbidium* orchids, and cockscomb (*Celosia argentea*) with its velvety texture and ruby intensity. The delicate glory lily (*Gloriosa superba*), equally glorious lilies such as blood lily (*Haemanthus*), and other *Lilii* come in many shades of pink, red, and coral. Pink and red carnations (*Dianthus*) and maroon chrysanthemums are not only perky and spicy in scent, they are long lasting. Amaranthus is a wonderful flower for Christmas arrangements and comes in an upright variety (*Amaranthus hypochondriacus*) as well as the hanging tassel type known as love-lies-bleeding (*A. caudatus*). Ginger heliconia (*Heliconia*) and *Leucosperum* both present lovely hues of red. For sheer theatricality, look for painter's palettes (*Anthurium*), which come in

red, pink, and white. Equally exotic, miniature pineapples (*Ananas comosus*)—look for ones blushed with red—are classic symbols of welcome.

White flowers abound, including lilies, amaryllis, carnations, chrysanthemums, and many of the other species that also appear in shades of red and pink. White blossoms are likely to be especially aromatic, probably because they have to rely on scent rather than color to attract the insects that pollinate all flowers. The

Before arranging flowers, recut stems and give blossoms a drink of lukewarm (not ice-cold) water.

• • •

Cut rose stems on a forty-five-degree angle, split hard stems such as cyclamen with a knife, and flatten woody stems such as camellia or flowering quince with a hammer.

• • •

To make roses last longer, wrap the heads in paper to protect them and plunge the ends of the stems into boiling water for a few minutes.

• • •

Be sure to purchase peonies and roses two days before you need them so that they will have opened fully by the time your guests arrive. Tulips need a day to open properly.

• • •

To ensure that the long, hollow stems of amaryllis do not break or bend, insert a cane into the stem. You can also fill the stems with water and plug with a cotton ball to extend their life.

• • •

Poinsettia has a milky sap that can cloud water. When using in cut arrangements, seal the stem end by holding it over a match or lighter for a minute.

• • •

Remove all leaves and branches that will fall below the water-line so they will not rot and muddy the water. Leave foliage above the waterline to enhance the arrangement.

• • •

Instead of stones or marbles, place the following in the bottom of glass containers holding flowers: shells, horse chestnuts, lady apples, cranberries, whole kumquats, sliced star fruit, lemons, or limes.

• • •

Ripening fruit emits ethylene gas, which can retard blooms, so keep flowers away from fruit, both on a table and, in the case of bulbs, in the fridge.

• • •

A floral arrangement should be at least one and a half and often two times as tall as the container. Use shallow containers for large blooms such as lilies or peonies with the stems cut short. Use straight-sided vessels for stiff branches and stems such as larkspur, delphinium, or gladiolas. Tumbler-style vases with narrow bases and wider mouths are better suited to stems such as tulips, lilac, and roses that cascade gently.

sweet aromas of narcissus and hyacinth bulbs forced into early bloom herald the coming of spring even during the midwinter celebration. The sweet scents of camellias and gardenias are equally heady. Stephanotis, whose scented waxy blooms are often used for weddings, is another superb holiday flower. Some florists stock out-of-season white flowers such as ranunculus, sweet peas, Queen Anne's lace, and lily of the valley.

Although green is typically thought of as the hue for foliage, there are a surprising number of green flowers, which complement others of any color, and can especially soften the harshness of red blooms. Before a hydrangea matures to cream, blue, pink, or even red, it often displays a lovely shade of chartreuse.

Other common flowers that offer up a pale green version include chrysanthemum, decorative onions (*Allium*), and hellebore. In addition, if green blooms intrigue you, look for feathery lady's-mantle (*Alchemilla*), *Cymbidium* orchids, varieties of *Protea*, spurge (*Euphorbia myrsinites*), star-of-Bethlehem, *Moluccella laevis*, and yellow-green *Hypericum*.

While red, white, and green may be Christmas classics, by no means should you feel you must limit your floral selection to these conventional colors. The flower world abounds with blues and yellows, oranges and purples that interject a note of unexpected beauty into your festivities. Just as I would never eliminate all the colors of the rainbow from my glass ornaments, I urge you to use whatever blossoms appeal to you.

RIGHT: **Marlo Phillips used a silver urn as the base for this extravagant arrangement. Ophelia hybrid tea roses drape gracefully over the sides, while Radko "Poinsettia" finials fill the center.** BELOW: **Cut-crystal bowls cradle fresh-cut white hydrangeas that echo the shape of the containers. A dried hydrangea topiary takes center stage.**

AT THE HEARTH

WE MAY RELY ON FOSSIL FUELS TO HEAT OUR HOUSES,
BUT NO MATTER HOW ADVANCED OUR TECHNOLOGY,
NOTHING CAN REPLACE THE LURE OF A CRACKLING
FIRE LIGHTING UP THE ROOM AND FILLING IT
WITH THE AROMA OF WOOD SMOKE. THE MYTHIC
IMPORTANCE OF THE HEARTH IS AS OLD AS MANKIND.
DARKNESS WAS SIMPLY A FACT OF LIFE UNTIL MAN
LEARNED TO MAKE AND SUSTAIN FIRE, WHEN HE
REALIZED HE ALSO POSSESSED SOME CONTROL OVER
THE FORCES OF DARKNESS. A MANIFESTATION OF THE
SUN THE ANCIENTS WORSHIPED, FIRE REPRESENTED
LIGHT, HOPE, EVEN LIFE ITSELF. IN THE MINDS AND
HEARTS OF OUR ANCIENT FOREBEARS, FIRE TRULY
MUST HAVE BEEN A GIFT FROM THE GODS.

o it is not surprising that fireplaces answer needs more intangible than our mere desire for physical warmth. Lighting a fire indoors evokes something basic in human nature, perhaps an atavistic memory of our days as cave dwellers. We are drawn to the warmth and glow of coals and the scent of burning wood. A roaring fire suggests comfort, safety, and all the traditional virtues of home. It also conjures up both romantic and convivial emotions. Much of our Christmas imagery centers on the hearth: It is the perfect setting for the social pleasures of drinking a toast, roasting chestnuts, or reminiscing about Christmases past. And solitary contemplation of the dancing flames seems to naturally evoke thoughts of the cycles of life and death that are inherent to this season. Like so much Christmas iconography, the symbolism that surrounds the fireplace is a blend of pagan rituals and Christian legends. For example, in Norse mythology, Hertha, the goddess of home and domesticity, descended into a home through the smoke in a fireplace; her coming brought good fortune to a family. Add in the concept of the medieval harvest festival and the banqueting hall complete with commodious hearth garlanded with nature's bounty. Then sprinkle in a large dose of Victorian sentiment and these many threads come together in a magnificent tapestry of ideas for holiday decorations. No wonder we want to make this natural focal point made even more visually engaging.

PREVIOUS PAGE: **A mantelpiece holds a collection of *Kugels* and mercury glass.** ABOVE: **Roasted chestnuts by the fire.** OPPOSITE: **With a magnificent tree reflected in the mirror and a crystal chandelier decked out with a large *Kugel*, this chimney-breast needs minimal decoration: gilded angel candleholders, red candles, and a few sprigs of greenery.**

Yule Log Lore

One of the many holiday customs associated with the hearth is the Yule log, a powerful symbol of renewal and regeneration originated by the Druids. Long before the birth of Christ, the peoples of northern Europe considered the Yule log the symbol of the undying Sun, which would return light and warmth to them in the spring. The mighty log was thought to bring good fortune and

ABOVE: **A vintage teddy embraces a Christmas cracker; "Cookie Cutter Frostie" keeps an eye on things.**

fertility to the household. As with so many other pagan customs, the Christian leaders absorbed this ancient tradition into the practice of the new religions so converts would not have to give up a much-loved ritual. And ritual it was.

Preferably from an oak or a fruit-bearing tree such as an apple, the log was selected months before the holidays to ensure that it would be thoroughly dry in order to burn easily and brightly. People believed that whoever participated in bringing in the "Christmas brand" would be protected from witchcraft in the year to come. So whole families and their servants would go out to the forest to drag in the log, which would be draped in garlands. It was important to find a log large enough to burn for the twelve days of the holiday. Before being lit, the behemoth would be ceremoniously carried around the room, anointed with wine, toasted, even kissed and serenaded. The new Yule log was then placed in the fireplace and lit with a brand remaining from the Yule log of the previous year. Tossing a sprig of holly into the fire was supposed to put an end to any bad luck suffered earlier in the year. By the time it had become part of the Christmas celebration, the log would not be brought into the house until Christmas Eve. On the twelfth day, tradition deemed that the fire be put out and remains of the Yule log kept as protection against lightning for the remainder of the year. Ashes from the log were used to fertilize fruit trees in the seasons that followed. Although we usually no longer burn a special Yule log, the tradition persists in the form of a cheery fire in the hearth at holiday time.

Stockings to Fill

The idea of hanging stockings by the fireplace originated with the legend of the historical figure now known as St. Nicholas, who was born in Asia Minor late in the third century. His parents, devout Christians, left him their fortune, which he used to do good anonymously. As the legend goes, three impoverished sisters had despaired of finding husbands because they were without dowries. Hearing of their plight, St. Nicholas tossed bags of gold in a window of the women's house at night while they slept. One bag fell into a stocking hanging by the fire to dry. In the morning the young women awoke to find their fortunes and opportunities had dramatically improved. Among other honors, St. Nicholas is now known as the patron of marriageable girls.

From this oft-told tale evolved the idea of Santa improbably squeezing down a chimney to leave gifts for children in stockings hung by the chimney. In 1809, Washington Irving's *A History of New York* mentioned the custom. A children's book published in 1821 titled *A New Year's Present* associated Santa Claus with Christmas stockings. Sixteen years later artist Robert Walker Weir depicted Santa standing by a fireplace hung with stockings. Two socks were stuffed with goodies, another filled only with switches, blending another legend of a devil-like antihero called variously Black Pete, Krampus, or Hans Trapp, who accompanied Santa on his travels, leaving only coal and switches for naughty

HUNG BY THE CHIMNEY WITH CARE

A ritual of childhood is hanging your stockings by the fireplace on Christmas Eve. Whether it was one of your father's cast-off argyles, a gaudy red-and-white felt job, or perhaps a one-of-a-kind beauty knitted by a loving relative, the expectation was the same: that a limp, empty piece of fabric would be transformed by morning into a bulging receptacle of delights. Stockings come in a wonderful array of knitted Nordic designs, felt fantasies, plus needlepoint, embroidery, and even satin styles.

- Stockings must be ample in size—not only to accommodate more goodies, but so that they look in scale to the fireplace. The space for tiny stockings is on the tree or a wreath, not the mantel.
- If you are going to decorate with stockings—meaning they will be up for the duration of the season—be sure to stuff them with tissue paper and include a few decorations spilling out the top. They should look as bountiful as the spirit of the holiday. You can always replace the tissue and decorative items with gifts on Christmas Eve.
- To secure stockings to the underside of the mantel, use heavy-duty cup hooks or C-hooks. You can also purchase decorative brass hangers designed to attach to the mantel without having to hammer in a nail or screw in a hook. These come in particularly handy with stone mantels.

children. But it was the publication of the poem "A Visit from St. Nicholas," by Clement C. Moore, that engraved on our consciousness the custom of hanging stockings.

Another version of this custom evolved out of the seventeenth-century Dutch custom of leaving out wooden shoes filled with carrots and hay on Christmas Eve for St. Nicholas's horse (Rudolph and the other reindeer are an American elaboration). In return, Santa would fill the shoes with treats for the household's children. German immigrants brought that custom with them to the New World.

A Natural Focal Point

Even absent all these delightful legends and customs, the fireplace presents a natural canvas for creativity. In addition to the expanse offered by the chimneybreast itself, the mantel, the surround, and even the chimney box beckon for ornamentation. As with all Christmas décor, take your cues from the architecture itself. A refined reproduction Adam mantelpiece in a neocolonial house will clearly suggest different motifs from a river rock chimneybreast in a Colorado ski lodge. Scale is important as well. A broad expanse of wall or a wide mantel demands a large, lush arrangement. A lacy wreath of bittersweet hung above a massive fireplace will get lost. On the other hand, an elaborate swag in Della Robbia style might overwhelm a delicate mantel and surround. Decorations used elsewhere in the room (see "Deck the Halls," page 76, and "The Art of Display," page 138) also need to be considered when adorning the hearth.

ABOVE: **Wooden clogs filled with straw and gifts stand in for stockings hearthside.** OPPOSITE: **Bittersweet tucked into a willow wreath adds color and freeform abandon. A pair of antique dog doorstops sports jaunty bows.**

Above It All

Whether it is a flat expanse of wall or an angled or curved projection above the fireplace, the chimneybreast is usually of relatively generous size. There are two general approaches you can take in this area. One is to accent an attractive, properly scaled mirror or piece of art hanging on the chimneybreast with greenery and other holiday decorations. You may want to replace a painting of a floral subject with a winter scene just for the holidays. The classic, formal treatment is to enhance the frame with a garland of greenery, often in concert with paired

sconces, vases, or other decorations. A mirror also offers opportunities for playing with reflected light and imagery. Or, for a holiday change of pace, you could cover the entire frame with polystyrene and stud it with bouquets of wheat, seedpods, pomanders, and nuts or use another naturalistic treatment.

The other approach is to remove that painting or mirror and hang, for example, an oversize wreath that is itself a work of art. Ratchet up that impact by combining the wreath with a garland that drops gracefully to either side, perhaps caught with a bunch of ribbons and ornaments before cascading to the floor on either side of the fireplace surround. Or, exploit the power of repetition with three wreaths arrayed across the chimneybreast, linked with satin ribbons. Another dramatic approach that works well when the fireplace is centered on the wall is to swag a plump garland of greenery from the middle of the chimneybreast and across the wall, catching it up every few feet with glorious bows.

Assuming the Mantel

A mantel is integral to the hearth. A mantel serves as a stage for countless decorations and is also a relatively safe spot for precious possessions. Take into consideration the depth of your mantel, which could limit what you place on it. I love to mass an army of candles on the mantel, mixing heights and diameters for a blaze of light. Wrap ivy around the bases or tuck in bits of other greenery. If you have a collection of holiday articles, this might be the perfect place to display them (see "The Art of Display," page 138). You can also use the mantel to build up a scene, such as a magical winter village, complete with tiny buildings, bottlebrush trees, sleighs and reindeer.

But you don't need special Christmas collectibles to display on the mantel. Work with what you already have; say, a pair of cranberry-glass pitchers, or a collection of mercury-glass vases filled with seasonal flowers and berries. This

ABOVE LEFT: **Beaded "Jingle Star" and "Guiding Star" are suspended on organdy ribbons from the fire screen.** ABOVE RIGHT: **A formal fireplace gets the full treatment. On the mantel, bouquets of Festiva peonies and golden candles in a crystal candelabra dressed with sprigs of yew flank a superb bull's-eye mirror. The boxwood garland is wrapped in ribbon and caught with lush arrangements of glass fruit ornaments.**

ABOVE: **Maidenhair and mother ferns and myrtle topiaries fill a nonworking firebox.** OPPOSITE: **Pyramidal birch twig topiaries are wrapped with grape vines and studded with fresh gardenias in plastic vials. White birch logs and pillar candles add to the woodsy drama.**

narrow proscenium lends itself to all sorts of floral and fruit arrangements. Or snuggle half-round topiaries made from lady apples, lemon leaves, and cranberries against the wall. Center a dramatic spray of white roses, variegated holly, and baby's breath with tendrils of ivy spilling out, then anchor each end with potted candy-cane amaryllis. Lay boughs of fir on the mantel, then artfully arrange chartreuse-green quinces, pyracantha berries, and perfect yellow pears accented with beeswax columns. Or secure a garland of bay leaves, eucalyptus, or other greens at either corner, then let it spill over to either side, catching up the corners with bunches of miniature pineapples and berries tied in bows.

With an area so prominent, your efforts should be bold. More is always better; bigger has more impact. Line up a dozen glass apples on the mantel, not five; twenty snowglobes, not three. Use a battalion of candles in a variety of sizes rather than a matched pair standing stiffly at attention. Repetition has its own momentum: A collection of graduated copper-luster pitchers, each holding a flower or sprig of holly, achieves the visual "grab" of a single, larger object. In asymmetrical arrangements, odd numbers of objects are more interesting. Five nutcrackers accentuate the similarities and differences among them; with four, your eye tries to pair them off.

A charming European custom is to trim the mantelpiece with a narrow piece of fabric tacked to hang a few inches over the edge. Normally, such an apron is made of lace or linen, but at holiday time it could just as easily be tartan or red felt, perhaps in a sawtooth pattern. (Be sure to hang the apron well out of reach of the firebox.)

Surrounded with Beauty

The third area of the hearth that lends itself to decoration is the surround, the wood or stone area adjacent to the firebox and below the mantel. Many decorations—a swagged garland, for example—may involve both the mantel and the surround; others are confined to the surround. A pair of pinecone topiaries placed to either side of the fireplace are independent elements, although as always it is advisable to relate them to a design component on the mantel. A gar-

SAFETY TIPS

- Make sure the Christmas tree and any other cut greens are well out of reach of the fireplace.
- No decoration on the mantel or surround should get too close to the firebox. Only noncombustible decorations should hang in front of the firebox.
- Never burn wrapping paper or colored newsprint. Both contain inks that could release pollutants into the air.
- Do not dispose of pine needles or any evergreen boughs in the fireplace. They burn so quickly, they could throw sparks into the room, or cause a fire in your chimney or outdoors.
- Never leave a fire unattended.
- Always use a properly fitted mesh or glass fire screen to deflect flying sparks and embers.

land of Indian corn, or cranberries interspersed with acorns, swagged from side to side under the mantel and then dropping from either side of the surround, is another example.

Boxed In

Well before the holidays, make an appraisal of your fireplace gear. Is it time for some new andirons or a handsome fire screen? Andirons, also called firedogs, come in gleaming brass or graphic cast or wrought iron. A handsome fire screen accentuates the inherent beauty of the dancing flames. At Christmastime, screens that depict fir trees, leaping stags, or other Nordic-inspired themes are particularly appropriate. Other screens are neutral enough to allow you to wire flat ornaments (made of metal or glass or another noncombustible material) to the fire screen. When a fire is lighted, the effect can be wonderfully dramatic. Alternatively, you could hang ornaments on fishing line or ribbons from the mantel at staggered heights.

If you have a nonworking fireplace, there's no reason to give in to the black-hole complex. To simulate the look of a blaze in a nonfunctional firebox, place a metal tray inside, then fill it with lots of column candles or votives. One surprising but effective idea is to hang a wreath from the mantel so that it hangs in front of the firebox. Illuminated with tiny lights, it provides its own nighttime magic. You can, of course, also place a container in the firebox filled with greenery, flowers, pinecones, or whatever else you wish. A bundle of white-birch logs is always handsome. Or, hang a few yards of wonderful red damask in front of the opening and hang ornaments from the mantel. A low fireplace screen covered in marbleized paper or mirrors could also prove a dramatic backdrop.

THE SCENT OF CHRISTMAS

The scent of a wood-burning fire is always pleasurable, but to make the blaze even more aromatic, burn fruit-woods such as apple, cherry, and mulberry; pinyon or hickory also each have their own distinct scent. Or toss in sticks of cinnamon, dried citrus peels, or bundles of lavender and sage. To make your own firestarters, dip pinecones in paraffin. You can also add scented oils to the paraffin. Or bundle together dried twigs, eucalyptus sprigs, and cinnamon sticks. Tie in a neat bunch with raffia or sisal rope; while these natural firestarter bundles wait in a basket by the fireside, they serve as pretty decorations. There are also products available that scent a fire or color the flames in dramatic colors, but two homemade solutions are to sprinkle salts of copper chloride (available at a hardware store) on logs for blue and green flames; common table salt provides brilliant yellow flames. You can also sprinkle a few drops of an essential oil, such as pine, juniper, orange, or sage, on balled-up newspapers for added aroma.

WAXEN WONDERS

WHERE ONCE CANDLES were essential to banish darkness, today we treasure them for the romantic and dramatic atmosphere they provide. There is something about the glow of a flickering golden flame that transforms any setting. Candles' connection to prayer and meditation add a spiritual dimension as well. Ironically, now that we no longer need them every day, candles have become symbols of elegance and leisure, and a significant decorating accessory. But candles offer more than superficial beauty. They are imbued with meaning that an electric bulb can never replace, partly because they hail from antiquity and have long been associated with Christmas festivities.

Candles are regarded universally as the symbol of the soul, and they figure in religious rituals around the world. In the Christian faith, the candle is a symbol for Christ, the light of the world. Placing a candle in the window during the twelve days of Christmas is an old Irish custom, a symbolic guide for Mary and Joseph—and all lost souls—to find their way. At Hanukkah, the Jewish festival of lights, the nine-branched candelabrum called a menorah commemorates the reclaiming of the temple in Jerusalem from the Syrians in 165 B.C. During the siege, though there was only enough oil used for light to last one day, the stores of oil miraculously lasted eight days. Now, at each sundown

OPPOSITE: **The candle's warmth enhances the scent of gardenias floating in a pressed-glass punch bowl.** ABOVE: **Holly and eucalyptus berries and spruce frame a "Peace on Earth" candle that imitates a glass ornament of the same name. Rusted metal lanterns ramp up the exotic look.**

No matter what container you use, melt the bottom of the candle or use floral clay to secure the base. Use containers in multiples and stagger heights and widths of candles for maximum effect.

• • •

Place column candles in clay flowerpots. Leave the pots natural, paint them, or cover with gold leaf.

• • •

Bring in your outdoor metal lanterns. Those with decorative cut-outs offer wonderful light play.

• • •

Use mismatched glasses and goblets to hold votives.

• • •

Eggcups, teacups, saltcellars, Chinese soup bowls, and tin pastry molds also make unconventional holders.

• • •

Glass hurricanes add shimmer along with safety. Faceted or etched examples refract light especially well.

• • •

Hollowed-out mini pumpkins, gourds, apples, avocados, and even cabbages are naturals to hold votives.

• • •

Place larger columns on pieces of slate or marble.

during the eight days of Hanukkah, a ninth candle called a *shamash* is used to ritually ignite each candle in turn until all eight are lit. A similar tradition exists in the African American midwinter holiday called Kwanza, which centers on the lighting of seven candles, each symbolizing a different principle or ethic. Likewise, during the Christian Advent, on each of the four Sundays before Christmas, one more taper is successively lighted on the Advent wreath.

Incredible Choices

Although beeswax candles have been found in Egyptian tombs dating back to 3,000 B.C., clay and bronze candleholders that date to a millennium earlier prove that the candle existed even then. Most candles were once made from tallow, or rendered animal fat. Today, the average candle is made of paraffin, a by-product of the petro-chemical industry.

The longest-lasting and cleanest-burning candles are crafted of beeswax, some made from sheets of wax imprinted with the pattern of the honeycomb and rolled around a wick, and others molded or formed into tapers. Remarkably, it takes about 160,000 bees to produce the 60 pounds of

ABOVE: **Next to a planter made by hand from Spanish pinecones, pillar candles perch on birch log lengths.** OPPOSITE: **Brass candlesticks take on holiday airs fitted with red candles and placed on a sprinkling of rose petals among loosely arranged glass garlands.**

honey that in turn yield a pound of beeswax. No wonder in olden days, beeswax was considered a luxury affordable only to the nobility and the clergy; common folk relied on tallow candles. Indeed, beeswax was so precious it was once used as currency. Beeswax candles remain the most costly today.

Other natural sources of wax include the coatings of bayberries, tallow tree berries, wax myrtle, wax palm, and jojoba nuts, among others. Most candles are machine made, although hand-dipped or hand-twisted or molded ones that reveal the hand of the artisan are widely available.

The sheer variety of candles available proves how popular they are. In addition to classic white or ecru tapers and columns, candles can be found in more colors than a box of crayons. When it comes to design, tapers are crafted by dipping a wick repeatedly into hot wax, allowing them to harden between dips, which creates the characteristic sloped shape; tapers may be twisted or even braided while still warm into various shapes. Freestanding pillars can be circular, square, or star shaped. Molded candles that mimic snowballs, ornaments, Christmas trees, angels, and Santa Claus playfully acknowledge the season. Votives, once used primarily in houses of worship, come in myriad colors and scents, and can be paired with wonderful containers made of glass, crystal, china, or metal. Floating candles are shallow shapes designed to float in a bowl of water. Two recent trends are large pillars with several wicks and viscous gel candles that burn

Lighting Lingo

Pillar This freestanding candle is usually tall and cylindrical, but can also be made into other shapes such as a square, a hexagon, a triangle, a star, or a heart. Pillars should be burned on a flat holder.

• • •

Taper A thin, usually tall candle that gradually tapers at the top and is designed to fit into a candleholder.

• • •

Column A slim shape with perfectly straight sides (unlike a taper). Some have points that are sharply defined like a pencil point. The base may be pegged or simply flush with the rest of the candle to fit into a candleholder.

• • •

Votive A small candle designed to sit in a holder or cup. It will completely liquefy as it burns, essentially becoming a small container candle.

• • •

Tea light Also known as a night light. Smaller than a votive, it comes in an aluminum or plastic cup and is usually sold in multiples.

• • •

Container In addition to votives in containers, candles may be formed in candy jars, seashells, tin canisters, or myriad other containers.

• • •

Novelty candles These irregularly shaped, freestanding candles may be molded or sculpted into an endless variety of forms. Because they burn unevenly, they are perhaps better to use for display purposes only.

Store candles out of direct sunlight and away from heat.

• • •

If the proportion of wax and wick is correct, a candle should be dripless. If you are not sure, place them in the freezer for an hour or two before lighting.

• • •

Always trim a new candle's wick before lighting. Keep the wick trimmed to ¼ inch to avoid smoking.

• • •

Secure the candle to the holder with floral clay or rubber candle grips. Or simply dip the candle base in hot water for a few seconds until the wax is soft enough to conform tightly to the cup in the candleholder.

• • •

Make sure candles are not too close to greenery, ribbons, or other flammables, or remove the trimmings when the candle has burned down to a dangerous level.

• • •

A small amount of water under the candle in a glass or china votive holder will keep it from overheating and breaking the container.

• • •

Do not place lit candles in a draft. They will burn too quickly and will drip. Or use hurricane shades.

• • •

Protect tables or cloths from drips by using bobèches between the candle and the holder or by placing a small plate under the candle holder.

• • •

Do not leave the room with candles burning, and never leave children or pets unattended around lit candles.

• • •

Always use a candle snifter to extinguish flame.

with wonderful luminosity.

The heat generated by the flame can release aromas in candles. Good holiday scents include bayberry, rosemary, balsam, pine, cinnamon, frankincense, peppermint, or cranberry. Aromatherapy candles, made with blends of essential oils rather than fragrant scents (which may be artificial), claim to reduce stress, enhance a certain state of mind, or even heal.

Designing with Light

Although we no longer put candles on our trees, placing them just about anywhere else is fair game. Candles work synergistically with greenery, fruit, collectibles, and any other decorative grouping. Traditionally, candlesticks or candelabra are placed on dining tables, yet using a votive candleholder at each place setting is also a nice touch. Feel free to mix heights, containers, and types of candle. For reflected glory, place candles in front of a mirror and near glass ornaments, cut crystal, silver, and other light-catching and -reflecting surfaces. Even if you are a proponent of less is more, candles are one case where the more is definitely the merrier. Here are some other ideas:

• Gather a group of candles on a metal tray and place it on a table or in an unused fireplace. Special holders can support eight or more staggered pillars.

• Intersperse a collection of brass, silver, or crystal candlesticks with votives.

• Place glass ornaments, pinecones, potpourri,

OPPOSITE: **A humble artichoke morphs into an elegant votive candleholder.** ABOVE: **Glass icicles tied to the bases of the classic white pillar candles raise the sparkle quotient. Like the candlesticks, the cut-crystal vase holding orange calla lilies is by Val Saint Lambert.**

or other decorative items in a glass hurricane surrounding a tall column candle.

• Glue pinecones and berries to the base of a thick pillar candle.

• Tuck votive holders into hillocks of moss.

• Wrap low columns with cinnamon sticks or birch bark, then tie with raffia or ribbon.

• Hang ornaments or crystal chandelier drops from candelabra, or entwine candelabra with glass garlands or ivy.

THE ART OF DISPLAY

USING COLLECTIBLES AND OTHER FAVORITE THINGS
TO CREATE ARRANGEMENTS TAKES ON SPECIAL
MEANING AT CHRISTMASTIME. THESE VIGNETTES MAY
DELIGHT YOUR GUESTS AND ENCHANT YOUR
CHILDREN, BUT THEY ARE PRIMARILY A FORM OF
SELF-EXPRESSION—AND THAT MAKES THEIR CREATION
ALL THE MORE ENJOYABLE. YOUR CHRISTMAS TREE,
WREATHS, AND GARLANDS ARE A JOY TO BEHOLD, BUT
THINK OF THESE SPECIAL HOLIDAY TABLEAUX AS THE
EQUIVALENT OF DESSERT IN THE CELEBRATORY MEAL
OF HOLIDAY DECORATING. ABOVE ALL, THE ART OF
DISPLAY IS A LICENSE TO PLAY, AN OPPORTUNITY FOR
ADULTS TO REVISIT THE TIME WHEN IF YOU COULD
IMAGINE IT, YOU COULD MAKE IT.

remember how you used to create fantasy environments as a child? One of my favorite school projects was to build a diorama. There is something magical about creating a world in miniature that appeals to me to this day. So get out your antique dolls, teddy bears, and other childhood treasures. Perch them on top of elaborately wrapped gift boxes and set them in the front hall. Assemble toy villages, trains, a dollhouse dusted with artificial snow, and a mirror to suggest a frozen lake.

Christmas memorabilia collector Fred Cannon knows how to reach deep into his inner child at holiday time. Each year Fred carefully sets up a wonderful miniature church made by his grandfather and surrounds it with "snow" and bottlebrush Christmas trees. On a mantelpiece Fred places a wooden Noah's Ark with dozens of beautifully carved and hand-painted animals lined up two by two. A charming crèche rests on another table. Surrounding himself with these miniatures, imbued with meaning that belies their toylike scale, never fails to remind him of the wonder and joy he felt as a child at Christmas. When I see a fabulous Christmas display in a store window on Fifth Avenue, I experience the same suspension of disbelief.

Arranging Christmas vignettes allows you to play another way, with displays that blur the line between the real and the artificial. For example, fill a rustic wooden bowl with blown-glass ornaments in the form of fall leaves. Mix real gourds with glass ears of corn and silver-plated acorns. I love to put my fruit and candy ornaments in glass jars on an open kitchen shelf and see how long it takes before a visitor realizes they are not edible.

To step back to the Victorian period, you might cover a table with a lace cloth, then set up a small Christmas tree or feather tree and adorn it with velvet bows, reproductions of Victorian Christmas cards, and party snappers.

PREVIOUS PAGE: **Radko fruit ornaments, sugared grapes, and cascading blooms of love-lies-bleeding set in a silver compote signify abundance.** ABOVE: **Noah and his wife survey the animal kingdom from their ark atop a marble mantel.** OPPOSITE: **Fred Cannon's grandfather made this chapel in part from cigar boxes. The wire fence was made to surround a Christmas tree.**

Blur the boundaries between indoors and out. When we were decorating a bay-window recess with clumps of moss and flowers, it suddenly occurred to us to bring a stone garden ornament inside. The little squirrel gave the tableau a whole new dimension of whimsy. Look around for cast-iron urns, small garden statuary, any item that could benefit from a period of hibernation inside.

Arranging beautiful objects to create something larger than the sum of their parts is one part gift and one part grit. Surprise is an important component of any display. Place seven Limoges boxes on a table and you have a collection; add a Battenberg-lace cloth and some delicate sprigs of greenery and you have created a pleasing tableau. But tuck a couple of the boxes into bird's nests, and you are thinking like a display artist. For a similar juxtaposition, plant a tabletop garden of decorative kale in elegant silver bowls. This unexpected pairing of components makes you look at them both in a whole new way.

Setting the Stage

There are three steps to follow when making a holiday display: Decide which surface to use as your staging ground, then what collections or other possessions you would like to display, and finally how you will accessorize them with ribbons, flowers, and the like. Your dining table calls out for a centerpiece, even one as simple as a bowl of flowers mixed with Christmas balls or a pair of pinecone topiaries. A centerpiece adds warmth to the room between meals and becomes an integral part of the environment when the table is set. We will look at centerpieces in detail below, but first look around your house for other tables that could benefit from a dose of holiday décor. Clear that pile of unread books, magazines, and newspapers off your coffee table and replace it with something that will make your heart soar. Instead of a small bowl of flowers or potpourri, think big, fantastical, dramatic. How about a fairy-tale woodland of club moss and votive candles, perhaps with some tiny wooden or cardboard houses with pine-needle-thatched roofs? (You will need several baking sheets under the moss to protect the table.) Pile antique *Kugels* in a footed silver bowl with some smaller ornaments spilling over the sides and scattered artfully around the table. Mix components. When that low bowl of potpourri is joined by a compote holding ribbon candy and glass garlands and a vase of tulips, the scene will come together

visually, even as it engages your other senses.

When "tablescaping," be sure to leave room for a guest to put down a glass or allow space for your eyeglasses on your bedside table. Your arrangements should enhance your life, not look like a department-store display. Seek out other surfaces, such as a chair by the front door, cubbyholes in a drop-front desk, or the sill over the kitchen sink, to decorate.

Circular tables made from medium-density fiberboard or plywood (the kind designed to be covered with a cloth), or a battered old table that has been banished to the garage, can easily transcend their humble origins. Have a piece of glass cut and beveled to fit the top and place it over a handsome fabric. A full-length covering will turn a flea-market find into Cinderella for the season. Look beyond the usual table covers to pieces of lace, silk scarves, quilts, and other beautifully patterned or textured fabrics. A small rug might do a stand-in role on a table. Be equally open-minded about color. Don't limit yourself to green and red. Instead, play with variants on the theme, combining cranberry with sage, aqua with burgundy, chartreuse with pale pink. And when it comes to tartans, don't stop with green and red plaids; explore the whole glorious Scottish spectrum.

ABOVE: **Oil lamps cast their gentle glow upon a wooden trough filled with "Mini Oak Frost" and "Mini Maple Frost" glass ornaments.** RIGHT: **A Lilliputian winter scene takes place in a corner cupboard, where baking soda frosted with iridescent glitter stands in for snow. The two-dimensional German figures, called "flats," are painted pot metal. The chalet in the center is an old music box.** FAR RIGHT: **Craftswoman Gladys Bolt made the manger, the nativity figures, and the Star-of-Bethlehem.**

Object Lesson

Whether you have dared to go bare with a gleaming, polished wood surface—or perhaps bare stone or glass—or have selected a fabric covering, the next step is to assemble the other components of your display. If you have been collecting holiday-related items, this is the occasion you have been waiting for. But even if you don't have a closet full of chalkware Santas or silvered glass reindeer, you probably have plenty of other items to mine for ideas. Almost all of us collect something, be it copper-luster pitchers, seashells, paperweights, Victorian tartan-ware boxes, Art Deco candlesticks, star-

shaped objects, or miniature houses. I love to bring out my many collections and arrange them in different ways at Christmastime. For example, blue-green McCoy pottery that normally holds African violets and cut flowers makes superb containers for my collection of vintage Shiny-Bright glass ornaments.

You will not be surprised to hear that I collect antique glass Christmas ornaments, many of which have inspired contemporary designs in the Radko line. But I also collect anything antique that has to do with Christmas (and other holidays): miniature bottlebrush trees, Santa Claus figures, nutcrackers, cards, and candy containers in the shapes of Santa and snowmen, to name a few. These treasures all form the basis of my Christmas vignettes.

In addition to vintage ornaments made of glass, pressed lithographed cardboard (called Dresdens), and cotton, fellow collector Fred Cannon has an impressive collection of St. Nicholas figures, known generally as Belsnickels. Fur-clad figures are further defined as Pelz Nichol; Buller Closs carries bells; Aschenclos, ashes. Some are made of chalkware, others carved wood, others pressed cardboard; some are antique, others made by contemporary artisans. One group of Belsnickels marches across the mantel in Fred's dining room. In his bedroom, another set ranges in size from about four inches to about a foot, all dressed almost identically. Wonderfully intricate handmade Santas populate the windowsills and tabletops. Also highly collectible and enormously engaging is Fred's battalion of celluloid Santas, which perches on glass shelves in a mirrored recess. The hundreds of red-and-white fellows are a marvelous example of the impact of multiples—actually multiples of multiples.

Throughout his house, whether it is a certain kind of ornament or perhaps Russian lacquer boxes decorated with winter scenes, or silver spoons with Christmas motifs, Fred frequently groups like with like for impact. In other places, he mixes items to create a scene, such as wonderfully detailed alpine villages complete with houses, trees, and tiny inhabitants. Christmas cards, advertising art depicting Santa, snowglobes, and tins with silk-screened holiday designs can also be part of handsome vignettes.

Even if you have no formal collections, as you look around your house at the things you have acquired over the years, you will no doubt begin to see connec-

ABOVE: "Holiday Blossom" ornaments were grafted onto faux foliage and planted in a moss-topped urn, while "Pretty Petals" nestle in a glass compote beneath an alabaster lamp base and festive fabric shade. RIGHT: A vase of not-yet-ripe winterberries, ribbon candy, and a scattering of glass ornaments are proof that even the most casual arrangement can establish holiday spirit. The Radko "Santa Bell" consorts with vintage globes. OPPOSITE: Rosebud topiaries and a "Grandmother's Garden" glass globe find they have something in common.

tions among them. Perhaps you are attracted to the mellow luster of brass. An arrangement of brass candlesticks, boxes, bowls, and even a few representational pieces, set on a bed of greens and accented with wine velvet ribbon, immediately takes on Christmas airs. You can also work with objects you don't think of as a collection, such as a group of gold-tooled, leather-bound books, or cut-crystal decanters that usually hang out on the bar.

Play with things that sparkle: silver, crystal beads, tinsel, glass, mother-of-pearl, mirrors, and lusterware. Dabble with color, perhaps a range of greens from sandblasted glass to anodized copper to majolica plates. Gather together a lacquered tray, a bowl, a vase, and some old playing cards that all display a particular shade of rust. Instead of a subject or color theme, deliberate juxtaposition is also powerful: The mirror-smooth surfaces and sheen of mercury glass are accentuated against the rough texture of pinecones.

Even if your cupboards are bare you can make wonderful holiday arrangements simply by visiting a crafts store and/or the greengrocer. If you live in the country, you may be able to find pinecones, boughs, and strips of white birch bark, berries, and other natural items free for the taking. Pineapples, the traditional symbol of hospitality, boldly colored oranges and lemons, and gleaming apples await your creative impulses. Grapes, pears, and apricots lend themselves to sugaring. Less conventional fruits, such as not-yet-ripe persimmons, figs, and quinces, and pinky-brown lichee nuts and light green Osage oranges, both with wonderfully textured surfaces, can be found at specialty grocers and well-stocked supermarkets. Fresh nectarines, clementines, and cranberries are usually readily available at holiday time, as are chestnuts, pecans, almonds, and walnuts in their shells. These fruits and many vegetables lend themselves to an infinite variety of arrangements.

On a Scale of Importance

Scale, the relative proportions of one object to another and of all objects within a space, is crucial to a successful arrangement. In general, it is boring to regard a collection of objects that are all the same size. Like Goldilocks's three bears, big, small, and in-between make for just right.

LITTLE THINGS MEAN A LOT

- Tuck Christmas cards, whether recently received, saved from previous years, or vintage Christmas memorabilia into picture frames, mirrors, or special card holders.
- Attach bells to ribbons and tie around doorknobs. Try mixing a few different-color ribbons and various-sized bells.
- Tie a jaunty tartan ribbon around the neck of a cast-iron dog doorstop.
- Make pomanders by hot-gluing star anise, bayberries, nuts, and cloves to a polystyrene globe. Display them in a handsome bowl with some cinnamon sticks and bay leaves.
- Clip glass bird ornaments to curtain rods, tiebacks, the edges of picture frames, and other unexpected places.
- Stockings are not just for the hearth. Hang them from doorknobs, on the post of a bed, on a wreath, even on the wall.

But if the larger items loom huge, the smaller items get lost or look silly. In the right context, small can be charming and intimate—a tiny boxwood heart wreath tied with a ribbon on the pillow of a guest bed, for example. But be careful not to clutter the house with lots of small arrangements. Your eye gets confused when it doesn't know where to look first, creating disquiet. Group small objects together so they read as one to solve imbalances in scale. Even larger objects benefit from multiplication. Five candy-cane amaryllis lined up on the top of a bookshelf provide impact; a single one looks lonely; two may look too matchy-matchy.

When there are several decorated areas in a room, create a focal point and go for all-out drama; let other arrangements elsewhere in the room play important supporting roles. That's why you may want to keep displays in the room with the Christmas tree to a minimum. Instead, focus on other spots, such as the foyer, the dining room, even the kitchen and bedrooms.

The Importance of Relationships

One hint for beginners is to relate each secondary display back to the primary arrangement. Say the focal point of your foyer is a pair of large orange trees hung with silvery glass-bead snowflakes. On the front door, you might hang a lemon-leaf wreath wired with clementines and encircled with a wide silver bow. On the hall table, you could fill a crystal bowl with clove-spiked orange pomanders and nectarines. Above this, beaded snowflakes could hang on a balsam-and-lemon-leaf garland that graces the mirror. Repeating the components of citrus leaves and fruits, stars, and silver, without duplicating any specific combination, creates both continuity and interest.

When creating tableaux with vegetables, don't just use only predictable ones like corn, pumpkins, and other winter squash. Play off the colors of Christmas with an arrangement of red peppers, ripe tomatoes, red cabbages, Brussels sprouts, artichokes, and bunches of parsley (in water to stay crisp). When used with man-made or machine-made objects, flowers, fruits and vegetables, leaves, greenery, berries, and other natural items add warmth and life.

Just as inanimate objects are vitalized by the addition of

BELOW: **Hand-painted Russian lacquer boxes, garnished with juniper, depict winter scenes with troikas, or sleighs.** OPPOSITE: **For a fantasy trip, a gingerbread cottage is landscaped with a forest of Radko "Gumdrop Trees" and other beaded fantasies.**

plants and other natural objects, gilding the proverbial lily adds another dimension to Nature's creations. Go ahead and gild or spray-paint pears, apples, nuts, and pinecones silver, gold, copper, or bronze. Tie ribbons to stems of grapes. Dust grapes and other fruits with sugar, which serves as natural glitter. (Since real grapes don't last long out of the refrigerator, you might want to use artificial grapes, which can be remarkably convincing. Some come already "sugared.")

The Center of It All

Winter festivals are all about celebrating Nature's bounty to ensure that fruitfulness will resume when spring rolls around again. In no way is this better represented than with an abundantly lush centerpiece. A dozen roses may impress a first date, but for your holiday table, think at least three dozen. If you are using topiaries as part of a centerpiece, go for eight or nine, not just two. If you are playing with a harvest theme, make sure you have heaps of gourds, ears of dried corn, and nuts. Professional stylists always claim that unless they have too much, they do not have enough, and I heartily subscribe to this theory. You may wind up piling a lot on the table and then judiciously removing some of the objects to achieve a pleasing result. But you never want to be in a position of having a meager look or awkward holes in an arrangement.

As in everything, balance is the key to a successful centerpiece. Keep your priorities straight. For example, a container should never overwhelm the flowers in it. Better to have too many flowers in a small vase than a skimpy bouquet in an impressive ewer. If you have a display of cake stands decked with fruit, make sure the flowers or greenery between them is low so they complement rather than compete—and that you create a rhythm of heights on the table.

Although the most common centerpiece is an arrangement of cut flowers, the idea of putting flowers in water dates back to no earlier than the beginning of the nineteenth century. Before that, flowers were often strewn over the table—as much for their perfume as for their beauty. Consider these possibilities:

- Curl a garland of mixed fresh evergreens down the center of the table; top with pinecones, acorns, red berries, and white roses in florist's vials.

- Fill a long, low bowl with beautifully wrapped gifts to distribute to your guests at the end of the evening. Or tuck in sprigs of greenery, gilded leaves and nuts, glittering garlands, and other festive decorations.

- Fill a silver bowl with ornaments, shells, and strings of faux pearls spilling over the edge. Surround with votive candles to heighten the play of reflection.

- Scatter crystals or pieces of rock candy around the table, entwined in ivy or another vine and interspersed with votive candles in crystal holders.

TOP MIDDLE: **Also made by the Daubs, the New World Santa is inspired by the classic Thomas Nast illustration depicting a jolly elf with a potbelly, a short coat, and pants tucked into his boots, holding a bundle of gifts.** ABOVE: **Originally mass-produced but now very collectible, early celluloid and later plastic Santas and elves cavort among wooden figures and a plastic reindeer.**

- Place an evergreen wreath on the table, with a thick candle in the center, then decorate with tiny lady apples, gilded nuts, berries, or small ornaments.
- Arrange raw asparagus, artichokes, zucchini, and red peppers in an edible centerpiece garnished with oregano, basil, and other herbs.
- Place a pair of topiaries—whether alive, composed of fruits or other natural materials, or frankly fake (made of candy or ornaments)—at either end of the table. Two groupings of several individual topiaries are even more powerful.
- Fill a straw cornucopia with fruit and nuts, or mix real produce with vegetable- and fruit-shaped ornaments. Add sheaves of wheat and pheasant feathers.
- Pile a compote or a plate stand high with Osage oranges, pomegranates, lichee nuts in their prickly shells, rose hips, whole walnuts, almonds encased in their velvety skins, or other exotic fruits. Tuck in grape leaves or glossy lemon leaves or trail ivy tendrils or Spanish moss over the sides for a finishing touch.

- For a forest fantasy, strew berries, sprigs of evergreen, pinecones, petals, and gilded acorns and leaves around a centerpiece of compatible materials.

- Heap flowers such as peonies and red roses (in glass vials) mixed with fruit and glass ornaments in a large, low bowl for an abundant, Renaissance look.

- Place live moss in a basket with a waterproof liner, tuck in tiny votives or tea lights and sprigs of greenery, and scatter around some red berries.

- "Plant" a couple of cherry or other fruit branches forced into bloom in gilded flowerpots. Or use bare branches and hang with small, well-spaced glass ornaments or garlands. Tie a beautiful bow around each pot.

- Place a mirror on the table, dust it with artificial snow, and create a miniature winter wonderland complete with tiny topiaries or brush trees.

Above all, feel free to experiment. You'll find that this "time-out" will relax you in the midst of your hectic holiday schedule.

LEFT: **This lush arrangement plays with our senses. Pears and pomegranates on a transferware platter offer taste; potpourri, scent. But in company with the pittosporum berries and patterns of wallpaper, napkin, and tablecloth, the visual reigns supreme.**

'TIS BETTER TO GIVE

To me, the best thing about receiving a gift is the element of surprise. Until the moment the paper is torn off and the gift revealed, the fantasy that it could be anything holds sway, just as it did when I was a child. In this way, wrapped gifts represent the mystery and sense of expecta-

Top this: A pair of decorative handmade mittens and a perfect sprig of holly transform a gift wrapped in tissue paper and a satin bow into a work of heart. Jingle bells and red raffia complement an amusing penguin-print paper.

tion that permeate the Christmas season. I actually love to prolong the unknown, to shake the box and try to figure out what's inside. Receiving a gift is almost like winning the jackpot. And beautiful wrapping can ennoble the humblest gift or personalize the most extravagant one.

Although people have long given gifts to each other—the ancient Romans gave sumptuous presents during the feast of Saturnalia—it was not until the Victorian era that gift-wrapping became commonplace. Wrapping presents is actually a skill that anyone can learn. Once you master cutting and folding paper and tying a neat bow, the fun of selecting colors, textures, and accents begins. My advice about gift-wrapping will not entail how to make the perfect bow or folded corner; there are plenty of magazine articles that provide step-by-step instructions. Instead, I want to inspire you to express your own creativity while making a presentation uniquely suited to the recipient.

It's a Wrap

The variety of papers suitable for Christmas gift-wrapping is enormous. I happen to love foils in shimmering gold, silver, copper, and bronze as well as metallic jewel tones. There are also won-

derful printed papers, handmade Japanese rice paper, sherbet-hued tissue paper, and more. I buy rolls or sheets of paper throughout the year, whenever I see them, rather than wait until the last minute.

Like a horse and carriage and love and marriage, every beautiful paper deserves to meet its ribbon match. You will find a wonderful selection of paper ribbons in stationery stores. Skip the classic curling ribbon; instead pick up twisted paper raffia, jute, and woven ribbons. You will probably find satin cord and French wired ribbon in taffeta, organza, and other materials. Wired ribbon allows even a complete butterfingers to create superb bows after a few tries. For other quality-fabric ribbons, head for the notions department of a crafts or sewing-supply store. There you should find wispy, translucent organza; fluid, shimmering satin in silk and rayon; and velvet and velour. Shimmering moiré makes stiff bows; grosgrain has a bit more flexibility. I often like to use two ribbons in contrasting colors or layer a narrow ribbon over a wider one.

Collect an array of solid-color ribbons, but be sure to stock up on some of the wonderful tartans, stripes, and other printed or woven designs. Stores that sell home-furnishing fabrics often

The Element of Surprise

Delight the recipient of a gift with one of these teasers that play with revealing and concealing. Delaying the moment when the gift is finally revealed only adds to the suspense.

• • •

Wrap a gift twice: once in, say, pink tissue paper, then again in plum-colored foil. Or, wrap in a patterned paper and cover with tulle or glassine to reveal the inner layer.

• • •

Wrap a small gift, such as a piece of jewelry, in a series of successively larger boxes, each covered in coordinated papers and ribbons.

have wonderful offerings of gimp, braid, and other upholstery trims that can work wonders as ribbons. Look also for milliners' fruit and flowers, silk leaves, upholstery tassels, or other notions that can provide a delightful finishing touch. You can also tie tiny ornaments or bells to the ends of ribbons. Simply fold the end of the ribbon into a point and secure with a dab of glue or a few stitches. Then wire or sew on the ornaments or bells.

An idea worth adapting from the Japanese is to use a beautiful fabric such as a hand-blocked cotton print or a silk brocade and tie it into a decorative cover for your gift. Or use hatboxes or other attractive containers in lieu of a transitory wrapping. Your environmentally conscious friends will especially appreciate this approach.

To Top It Off

Tags or small cards are always appropriate ways to designate the "to" and "from." Or, cut up old Christmas cards with pinking shears to make gift tags. Simply punch a hole with a hole punch and attach with a narrow ribbon. You can even use a leaf and write a short message with a gold marker. A special touch is to accent each gift with another tiny gift tied with ribbon. My favorite accent to use, of course, is a tiny glass ornament, but I also love to haunt flea markets and yard sales for unusual items. Among my recent finds were a copper-plated horse for an equestrian, a cup from a child's tea set for a tea-drinking friend, and a tiny vintage teddy bear.

When the gift that serves as a decoration hints at the gift inside, all the better. Under the little horse was a pair of handsome jodhpurs; the teacup topped a sampler of exotic teas; the teddy bear alluded to a biography of Theodore Roosevelt. Top off your wrapped gift with the added treat of a small toy, doll, or an old-fashioned Christmas cracker. Here are a few other ideas to stimulate your creative juices. Many can later be hung on the tree.

- Bend wired lametta tinsel into a star or other shape.
- A cookie can be an edible name tag. Or use mesh bags of foil-wrapped chocolate coins or candy canes.
- Go natural with sprigs of holly or juniper, pinecones, shells, cinnamon sticks, or a nosegay of dried rosebuds.
- Attach a fresh flower in a glass vial or a beautiful silk flower.
- In lieu of a label, attach a tiny picture frame with a photo of the recipient.

TOP LEFT: **Shaker wooden boxes need only a couple of candy canes and a tartan bow; a hatbox gets a lift with cellophane and cookies. Ribbon candy tops a matte gold paper, an orchid two packages clad in wallpaper, a beribboned pinecone a tin box.** LOWER LEFT: **Other toppers include starfish, ornaments (here "Petite Candy" and "Jolly Santa"), cinnamon sticks, and even dried starfish.** TOP RIGHT: **Pale green and red silk organza, green velvet, tricolor corded ribbons, satin with a picot edge, gold-and-white twisted cord, green plaid, and red-and-white and gold-and-white French wired ribbons only hint at the options.** LOWER RIGHT: **A collection of handmade and hand-printed papers include an open-weave hemp.**

THE GROANING BOARD

ANYONE WHO DOUBTS THAT FOOD HAS A SPIRITUAL COMPONENT SHOULD THINK OF THE ASSOCIATION OF EGGS WITH EASTER, OF PUMPKIN PIE WITH THANKSGIVING, OF CHOCOLATE WITH VALENTINE'S DAY. HOLIDAY FARE IS ESSENTIAL TO CELEBRATING CHRISTMAS, BUT ITS PRESENTATION CAN ELEVATE THE REPAST TO AN ART FORM. WHEN WE EAT THESE TRADITIONAL DISHES, WE NOURISH MORE THAN OUR BODIES, JUST AS DECORATING OUR HOMES WITH SEASONAL PRODUCE IMBUES THEM WITH SPIRIT. NO HOLIDAY IS AS RICH WITH FOODS HAVING SYMBOLIC MEANING AS IS CHRISTMAS, ALTHOUGH MANY OF THESE DISHES PREDATE THE CELEBRATION OF CHRIST'S BIRTH.

*L*ike decking our houses with greenery, giving presents, and lighting a Yule log, many of the foods we associate with Christmas have pagan origins. Plum pudding, for example, is reputed to be a Druid recipe. The Druids are also responsible for initiating the tradition of roasting a boar—or its head—after sacrificing the animal to the goddess Frigga at their winter festival. German *Springerle* (anise cookies) were originally baked to honor the Norse god Wotan and his horse.

But even as we continue these age-old traditions, we bring new meaning to them. Making a holiday meal and dressing the table are repeated year in and year out. Yet these activities are also forms of personal expression, like decorating a Christmas tree.

Every festival worth its salt involves a meal of one kind or another, but ancient winter celebrations, whose function was to placate the gods and ensure the return of fertility in the spring, were particularly food oriented. Our forebears would stage a mammoth winter feast to spiritually fortify themselves for the long dark months ahead. But these blowout feasts had a practical component as well. They took place at the very time when stores of food, including grain to feed the animals, would soon be limited. As a result, farmers usually had to butcher most of their stock. The menu would likely include roasted goose or turkey, suckling pig or boar's head, and beef. Roasts would be joined by baked goods and puddings scented with spices, enriched with preserved fruits and often marinated in spirits.

A remarkable number of these dishes have remained on the contemporary holiday table. My favorite Christmas dinner includes a roast bird of some sort—a turkey, a goose, or even a guinea hen, complete with crackling skin and gravy made from pan drippings. The aroma of a bird roasting in the oven speaks not just of the savory meal to come but of a home filled with family and friends, good conversation, and good vibrations. Any food seasoned with spices, especially cloves, also pushes all my Christmas-spirit buttons. These exotic flavorings literally give spice to life, and bring the essence of good food into focus.

PREVIOUS PAGE: **Tiffany's "Holiday" china rests on vintage sterling silver chargers. Linen buffet-size napkins stand in for place mats.** ABOVE: **A festive spray on the chair back beckons diners to table.** OPPOSITE: **A Radko Belsnickel adds a whimsical touch to a formal silver tea and coffee service.**

LEFT: **The dining room at Lyndhurst, a Gothic-style mansion once the home of 19th-century railroad magnate Jay Gould, is the setting for an extravagant Christmas dinner. Roping swagged from each corner of the room meets above the chandelier, which is ornamented with ribbons and dozens of Radko ornaments. On the table, topiaries made from glass grape ornaments share real estate with silver serving pieces and George III English candlesticks.**
BELOW: **Chair backs complement the overall décor.**

Classic Dishes

Many of the foods entwined with American Christmas celebrations appear to be of northern European origin, primarily German and English. But many of these foods had their antecedents in another culture. Gingerbread, for example, actually originated in the eastern Mediterranean and was brought to Europe at the end of the eleventh century, possibly by Crusaders returning from the holy wars. The word "gingerbread" is a corruption of the Old French word *gingebras*, which in turn came from the Latin word *zingeber*. Ginger preserves baked goods, which no doubt added to its popularity. In some locales, gingerbread was a soft cake; in others, a crisp, flat cookie, or even bread. Regardless, it was often formed into decorative shapes and topped with icing or confectioners' sugar. Gingerbread was frequently sold at medieval fairs, with various shapes associated with different seasons.

ABOVE: **Bûche de Noël, a classic French dessert served on Christmas Eve, is decorated to look like a Yule log.** OPPOSITE: **At the meal called *réveillon*, no fewer than 13 desserts are served, among them a cakelike bread called *pompe à l'huile, calissons d'Aix* in the shape of almonds, nougat, squares of quince paste, nuts, and fresh and dried fruits. A crown of pepperberries, eucalyptus, and dried hydrangea dresses up the wire chandelier.**

Nuremberg, Germany, the site of a *Christkindlmarkt* in December, became the gingerbread (or *Lebkuchen*) capital of the world, famous for its intricate gingerbread angels, hearts, wreaths, and more. Large pieces of *Lebkuchen* are used to build *Hexenhäusle*, or "witches' houses," inspired by the fairy tale of Hansel and Gretel. These charming creations were sometimes also called *Lebkuchenhäusel* and *Knusperhäuschen*, "houses for nibbling at."

The French were no slouches when it came to gingerbread. Dijon, Reims, and Paris were particularly known for their *pains d'épice*, or spiced bread. *Printen* molds, which may be up to three feet in length, are still used by Alsatian bakers to stamp a design on a special cookie called a *Printen*. German settlers brought gingerbread recipes to this country; regional variations include the use of such ingredients as molasses and maple syrup. Later Scandinavian settlers introduced their own versions in cookies such as *pepparkaker*. Regardless of recipe or shape, the sweet, spicy scent of gingerbread says Christmas.

Another Christmas classic, mincemeat pie, often known as "Christmas pie," originated more than five centuries ago. Originally, mincemeat consisted of chopped meat and suet, which was cooked with apples, dried fruits, spices, and

wine or brandy. The spices helped preserve the meat in the days before refrigeration. The pies were baked in an oblong shape to represent the manger at Bethlehem. Their latticed tops represented the stable's hayrack; the apples, the fertility of the season to come; and the spices, the gifts of the Wise Men. The dish was supposed to bring good luck, especially if you ate one for each of the twelve days of Christmas! Today's mincemeat pie is usually meatless and served as a dessert.

Plum pudding contains raisins, currants, and fruit peel, but, despite its name, no plums. (The name appears to have come from the word "plumb," which once meant "to rise or swell," as the raisins do when cooked.) Originally, plum pudding was served with meats as a first course. Later it evolved into a sweet, stiff pudding served for dessert with hard sauce. When the Puritans came to power in England, plum pudding and other holiday foods were banned, along with Christmas festivities themselves. But people continued to make these dishes; many are enjoyed, often in altered forms, to this day.

The Holiday Season

Today we tend to think of the Christmas season as lasting from Christmas Eve to New Year's Day. But in an earlier era, Christmas festivities embraced a six-week period, beginning with Advent, meaning the coming of Christ. Advent marks the official start of the Christmas season, commencing on the fourth Sunday before Christmas and ending at midnight on Christmas Eve. In many countries it is customary to hang an Advent wreath adorned with four candles horizontally from the ceiling or place it on a table. On the first Sunday of Advent, one candle is lighted, with another candle being lighted each successive Sunday until all four tapers are burning. Traditionally Advent was the time for making plum pudding and baked goods. Several saints' feast days take place during Advent, and certain dishes are associated with each. For example, St. Barbara, who shared her bread with the poor, is honored on December 4, so grain is traditionally used to decorate tables in the south of France.

European Catholics traditionally go to Mass on Christmas Eve. In France, where the evening is known as *réveillon*, an elegant meal is served after midnight

OPPOSITE: **In Italy it would be unthinkable to celebrate Christmas without a light fruitcake called** *panettone*, **here set out on the kitchen counter for breakfast. Eucalyptus, juniper, and bittersweet form an impromptu bouquet.**
ABOVE: **Gingerbread men and women lend conviviality to a simple twig wreath.**

ABOVE: An elegant Christmas breakfast table set for two includes an English George III teapot with a heater and a shell-shaped holder for toast. Coleport dishes and gilded English dessert cutlery rest on a brocade runner that overlies a damask tablecloth. The centerpiece is made from ornaments, velvet leaves, and faux berries.
RIGHT: A collection of Christmas-motif sterling-silver spoons includes one with a charming scene of stockings hung by the chimney molded into the bowl of the spoon. The forks, such as the one graced with Santa's head, are extremely rare.

Mass. The final course at *réveillon* is usually a *bûche de Noël*, a rich rolled sponge cake decorated with chocolate or mocha buttercream scored to simulate the bark of the Yule log. Another favorite Christmas dessert is *boule de neige*, which translates into "snowball," basically a bombe mold filled with ice cream that is decorated with rosettes of whipped cream. In the provinces of France, it is customary to serve thirteen desserts at *réveillon*, representing Christ and his twelve apostles. The repast is laid on three layered cloths to represent the Holy Trinity. Delicacies rely heavily on local and seasonal specialties and are always based on fruits, nuts, and honey. Dried figs, raisins, almonds, and hazelnuts are de rigueur and are called *les quatre-mendiants* because their muted colors suggest the robes worn by the four begging orders of Augustinians, Carmelites, Dominicans, and Franciscans. Another constant on the dessert card is a cakelike brioche made with olive oil, rosewater, and aniseed. Called *pompe à l'huile* (meaning it plumps up when dipped in wine), it must be broken with the hands instead of cut with a knife, or bad luck might ensue. Other dishes made from oranges, lemons, pears, plums, melons, dates, kumquats, quince paste, pinenuts, almonds, and walnuts usually turn up in one form or another; many of the dishes date from the Middle Ages. To ensure good fortune, you should sample each dish!

In most cultures the Christmas Eve meal is meatless, symbolizing that Christ, who shed his blood for mankind, was yet to be born on this date. Instead, the menu is usually based on a fish entrée. In Poland, the *Wigilia* (meaning "vigil supper") breaks a daylong fast that is eaten only after the youngest child in the family sights the first star in the evening sky. My heritage is Polish and French and my parents always followed the Polish custom of laying the Christmas Eve table with a linen cloth, over straw or hay to recall the manger in which Christ was born. Custom decrees that an even number of dishes be served to an uneven number of guests. One place is left empty for the Holy Spirit.

Epiphany, also known as Three Kings' Day, the Feast of the Magi, or Twelfth Night, marks the end of the twelve days of Christmas and commemorates the recognition of Jesus as the Son of God by the Wise Men. In many countries this is the day that gifts are exchanged. Often a single almond, bean, or tiny china doll is baked into a loaf of bread. Whoever finds the token in his or her serving

SHARE THE WEALTH

Part of the Christmas spirit includes sharing food with the poor and putting food out for animals. In Hungary, custom decrees that if a stranger appears at the door while the family is eating Christmas dinner, he is invited in. In France, farmers sometimes place a portion of their produce in front of their church crèche, later giving it to the needy. Germans and Scandinavians put out sheaves of grain for birds. Northern European children leave carrots and hay for St. Nicholas's horse. Spanish youngsters do the same for the Wise Men's camels. In the Tyrol, it used to be customary to set out a pan of milk for the Christ child and Mary. Why not incorporate some of these kind-spirited customs into your holiday practices?

is named the king or queen of the revelries that take place that evening.

Patriotic Fare

Most early Americans were no slouches when it came to Christmas dinner. The Puritans in New England may have been opposed to feasting and other Christmas festivities, but German immigrants had no such compunctions. Nor did Southerners, and Virginian George Washington celebrated with the best of them. Whenever possible, he would celebrate Christmas at Mount Vernon, pulling out all the stops at dinner. The custom of the time was to serve three courses and set the table with two tablecloths. The repast itself was said to include onion soup, oysters on the half shell, and broiled salt roe herring. A plethora of roasts—beef with Yorkshire pudding, suckling pig, turkey with chestnut stuffing—would have been accompanied by cold boiled beef with horseradish sauce and cold baked Virginia ham. For side dishes, guests would have had their choice of lima beans, baked acorn squash, baked celery with slivered almonds, hominy pudding, and candied sweet potatoes. Condiments included pickled watermelon rind, spiced peaches in brandy, and spiced cranberries. After this

impressive array, the table would be cleared and the top tablecloth removed. Dessert consisted of mincemeat, apple, and cherry pies, plus blancmange, plums in wine jelly, snowballs (whole

apples baked in pastry and served with hard sauce), Indian pudding, "Great Cake," ice cream, and plum pudding. After dessert, the second tablecloth would be whisked away and fruits, nuts, raisins, port, and Madeira were served on the polished wood surface.

ABOVE: Dinner for twelve at the governor of Connecticut's mansion pulls out all the stops. Tall Radko topiaries and a large ewer of roses and glass ornaments match the scale of the mahogany table and crystal chandelier. OPPOSITE: The octagonal decoupage plate, one of a dozen made for the governor by Scott Potter, each depicting a different fruit, sits on Haviland's "Parlon" gold-rimmed china. Flatware is "Francis I" by Reed & Barton, the crystal by William Yeoward, as are the saltcellars used to hold votive candles. Damask napkins are tied with a Radko ornament.

LEFT: **An intimate dinner for four strikes a rustic note. The tablecloth is used as a base for a bed of juniper sprays and pinecones. Topiaries made from berries and nuts on the side table and a rusted chandelier piled with greenery continue the woodsy theme.** ABOVE: **Sheryl Green sets a holiday table with Bernadaud's "Fivole" mismatched charger, dinner plate, and salad plate. A Santa figure and a glass pinecone, both by Radko, Christmas crackers, and pinecone candles supply holiday spirit. Sherbet is served in William Yeoward's "Marci" martini glass.** TOP RIGHT: **A white porcelain service plate showcases Radko's "Black Filigree" china. "Herringbone" stemware by Ralph Lauren adds sparkle. The linen napkin is caught up with a sprig of juniper.** RIGHT: **A rare antique Sèvres plate lends fancy airs to an inexpensive gold-tone service plate. Antique etched trumpet-shaped goblets and George III candlesticks complete the elegant setting.**

Today we take a more moderate approach to Christmas dinner, but even those of us who rarely cook or cook only simple fare the rest of the year find ourselves drawn into the kitchen to prepare traditional dishes. You may cook the same meals your mother and her mother before her did or you may create a meal that resonates for you because it alludes to your lineage even if it has been almost forgotten in practice.

Something Sweet

Baked goods are an important component of Christmas meals, and every country has its specialties, although differences may hinge on something as small as the use of a different spice or another fruit. Czechoslovakian Christmas bread is a braided loaf full of candied fruit and nuts. Ukrainian Christmas bread dispenses

Unconventional but wonderfully inviting, the centerpiece is half a white birch log drilled with holes into which plastic vials holding periwinkle hydrangeas, delphiniums in several colors, purple buddlaa, and blue veronica were inserted. Rose petals scatter over the tablecloth; slices of birch log serve as place mats and short lengths of log as candleholders.

with the fruit, instead being flavored with orange juice and topped with poppy seeds. Caraway buns called Wigs can be floated in the wassail bowl or served for breakfast on Christmas morning in Britain. Most locales include a fruitcake in their Christmas repertoire. Whether light or dark and whatever the exact ingredients, all fruitcakes are splashed with spirits and stored for weeks to improve their flavor.

The names of Christmas cookies are often as wonderful as their flavors. Consider a gingerbread snap, an anise drop, an almond shell, a hazelnut crescent, or a honey kiss. The spicy taste of bite-sized *Pfeffernüsse*, also known as peppernuts, made with black pepper, then rolled in confectioners' sugar, belies their miniature size. Molded and embossed *Springerle* (meaning "little jumpers") hearken back to Julfest, a pagan celebration in which Germanic tribes sacrificed animals to appease their gods. Poor people, unable to afford real animals, offered instead animal-shaped cookies as tokens. A cookie called Speculation gets its unusual name from its uncertain origin: The Danes, the Dutch, the Belgians, and the Germans all claim it for their own. Other cookies with evocative names include Neapolitan mustache, Finnish stags' antlers, and Pennsylvania Dutch snickerdoodles and belsnickels.

And then there are confections, including ribbon candy; candied citrus peel; red-and-white-striped peppermints; and, of course, candy canes. Balthazars, which hail from Eastern Europe and are named for the Ethiopian Wise Man, are a delicious confection of chocolate, walnuts, confectioners' sugar, rum, grated orange rind, and egg white. *Torrone,* as it is known in Italy, *turrón* in Spain, and nougat in France, is a chewy white candy made from almonds and hazelnuts.

Perhaps the most famous Christmas candy is marzipan, made from ground blanched almonds, sugar, beaten egg whites, and a flavoring such as orange-flower water. It can also be baked into cookies or used to fill pastries and breads. Marzipan originated in the Middle East and was brought back to Europe by the Crusaders in the form of coins called "marchpane," a corruption of an Arabic word. Tinted and shaped like fruits, vegetables, animals, and other figures, marzipan is an integral part of Christmas. And just in case you have ever lain awake at night

KNOW YOUR PLACE

Place cards, relics of a more gracious era, are a small but intimate touch on any table, making each guest feel unique and welcome. You can purchase place cards, often with a golden border or other decoration; or make your own, perhaps from handmade paper. Or turn a holly or bay leaf into a place marker with a gold ink pen. You can also use the gold leaves with which bakers decorate cakes. Porcelain place markers can be reused indefinitely. Just write in the name of your guest with a china marker.

One style of place card is folded so it perches on the table rather like a tiny tent. The other style is a simple rectangle that can be tucked into a place-card holder. These come in both silver and porcelain—a mismatched collection of antique holders could be a lovely addition to the table. Or, tuck each card into a pinecone or a bunch of holly or mistletoe. Place an individual flower at each place setting, perhaps in a florist's vial, tied with a velvet ribbon and a card tucked into the petals. Or snuggle the card into a wrapped party favor sitting on the plate or use an old-fashioned Christmas cracker embellished with the name of the guest.

wondering what a sugarplum is, it is a mixture of ground dates, figs, raisins, currants, nuts, crystallized ginger, and sugar rolled into balls.

The Gift of a Meal

Setting a beautiful table honors the food *and* your guests. Arranging the table is rather like staging a play, which is in turn another gift for your guests. So why not make the event as dramatic as possible, evoking joy, excitement, even mystery? How you set the table and arrange the sideboard can make the difference between a tasty meal and a magical and memorable experience. The accoutrements of china, silverware, glasses, serving dishes, tablecloths and napkins, candlesticks, and candles may be exquisite in their own right. But when combined with one another and a bounty of food and holiday decorations, they can become the stuff of high drama.

I love to introduce as much color and sparkle as possible. The reflective surfaces of silver, crystal, and porcelain are heightened with the soft glow of candlelight. I like to push the envelope by adding more glitter and glow in the form of glass ornaments; gilded fruit, nuts, or leaves; or even a sprinkle of glitter itself. Think of assembling a festive table much as you would plan a knockout outfit for a special occasion.

Material Considerations

Beyond having a table large enough to seat your guests and sufficient comfortable chairs, the tablecloth is the foundation of your holiday setting. Table linen—meaning all table coverings, including place mats and napkins—offers a texture and a background upon which all the other elements are placed. The cloth may be an opulent fabric such as silk brocade, satiny cotton damask, Madeira lace, or embroidered Irish linen, even humble homespun. White and ecru are always appropriate, but I urge you to use color as well, and not just classic red or green. In the red family, think of such rich shades as deep rose, plum, persimmon,

Vintage German candy containers all have a snowball base; some are topped with elves and other figures dressed in crepe-paper clothes, another with Santa's head. The punch bowl is Anglo-Irish 19th-century cut crystal, the candlesticks 18th-century Sheffield.

claret, and rust. Pale pink is extremely flattering to skin tones, especially with candlelight. Sage green, blue-green, apple green, and even chartreuse expand your green options. Dark colors can be a striking foil against white or light-colored china, and become more dramatic under candlelight. Fabrics shot with metallic threads add wonderful sheen to the setting. Unexpected but equally luxurious are jewel tones such as sapphire blue or amethyst. Consider two-tone damasks, paisleys, tartans, or checks if you like the lushness of a pattern-on-pattern effect or plan to use china with a simple pattern. Colorful embroidered cloths from places such as Mexico and Morocco can lend an exotic touch.

Layer one cloth over another for a luxe look. Netting, organza, or organdy over a woven fabric gives a wonderfully ethereal effect. For a more exotic approach, layer silk or wool shawls (sold as fashion accessories) over each other. On a round table, stagger square cloths over each other so that the eight corners

A serpentine-front side-board serves up three centerpieces. The faux peach and nut topiary is flanked by William Yeoward "Edwina" tiered cake stands, piled three high, where "Kissletoe" and other ornaments mix with faux peaches and real nuts and pinecones. Stephanotis blooms add scent. The Belgian mirror doubles the impact.

At a buffet table, ornaments compete with desserts for attention. A candelabra bears silver-colored candles while other candleholders serve as bases for Radko finials, more typically used as tree toppers. Radko "Pineapple," "Harlequin," "Poinsettia," "Royal Star," "French Regency," and "Star Fire" finials are further embellished with ribbons, faux flowers and leaves, and berries.

form evenly spaced points. Or remove one cloth after one course, as Martha Washington did at Mount Vernon: A pink cloth could be a delightful surprise under a bolder color for the dessert course. Or place a runner—with or without a tablecloth—the length of the table or two or three runners across the width of the table. This treatment allows you to show off a beautifully polished tabletop.

Achieve a similar effect by interweaving ribbons across the top of the table, perhaps with jingle bells attached to each end to hold them secure. Crystal chandelier drops, gilded acorns, or tiny glass ornaments would serve nicely as well. Place mats come in damask, linen, lace, and most other materials used for their tablecloth cousins.

Look at not just manufactured tablecloths but at fabric on the bolt. Silk damask used for curtains and upholstery is available in an array of wonderful colors. At most, you'll have to sew two or three seams to make a one-of-a-kind table covering. Or haunt flea markets for antique linen sheets or Marseilles cloth coverlets, both of which can make great table coverings, as do richly colored printed Indian bedspreads. For a totally different and totally glam look, how about gold or silver lamé? Any cloth should hang over the table at least twelve inches and preferably fifteen. For a very formal look, the cloth may hang almost to the floor; just be sure to leave enough of an opening for diners to position their legs comfortably under the table.

A table pad underneath the tablecloth protects the wood surface both from spills and from hot pots that could damage the finish. It also helps anchor the cloth on the table. Traditionally, formal tables were set with an undercloth called a "silence cloth" to mute the sound of cutlery and serving dishes hitting the table.

BUFFET STYLE

A buffet meal is traditionally laid out on a sideboard. (*Buffet* is French for "sideboard.") Buffet-style dining is often a good choice with a large crowd, but ideally there should still be a place at a table for each guest. If that is simply not possible, make sure that the menu takes into consideration that it is next to impossible to carve meat while perched on the edge of a sofa and that soup and foods such as creamed potatoes are invitations to disaster. Group chairs so people can converse easily with other guests. If these considerations are weighed, buffet dining can be relaxed and informal. Offering dessert buffet-style is a nice treat after sitting for an hour or more at the table.

RIGHT: **Classic pomanders, made by studding fresh oranges with whole cloves, take on a party look when the spices are arranged in a spiral or other design. Tied with ribbon, a trio dangles in front of a kitchen window.**

Napkins can either match the tablecloth or contrast with it. Either look is fine as long as the napkins are of the best quality. Just as pajamas made of pima cotton are delightful to sleep in, napkins made of 100 percent linen or cotton feel wonderful in your hand. They are also less likely than synthetics to hold stains. Damask napkins grow softer and more absorbent with each washing. (Along with gingerbread and marzipan, Crusaders brought back to Europe the exquisitely woven fabric from Damascus, which accounts for its name.) Napkins should be at least 20 inches square, but I prefer the expansiveness of a 22-inch one or even the 24-inch buffet-size napkin. When starched, linen napkins are crisp and

firm, allowing you to fold them in a decorative shape. Organza also lends itself to crisp folds. For a softer look, simply finger-press napkins into folds.

Damask and other cotton fabrics are softer, with a more fluid hand, ideal for tying with a piece of organza or satin ribbon. Or, use a length of tasseled golden braid, a sprig of holly, or a flower. An ornament tucked into or tied to a napkin makes a lovely party favor. You can also tuck napkins in glasses, catch them in a napkin ring, drape them over the plate and the edge of the table, or even hang them over the back of each chair.

LEFT: **Dessert at Christmas brunch beckons from milk-glass serving pieces. Oregonia tucked around an apple pie and a delicate sage-and-chili-pepper wreath add refreshing touches of greenery.**

Gingerbread and sugar cookies, candy canes, Christmas-colored candy corn, ribbon candy, and red and white Jordan almonds represent the delicious flavors children associate with the holiday. Peppermint-striped candles are just for fun.

Useful Decoration

If you have a set of Christmas china, you'll probably want to build your table setting around it, but plenty of other patterns will do as well. Feel free to mix other, compatible china patterns for salad or dessert plates.

Beneath your china, it is nice to use a service plate, also called a charger, which sits on the table before dinner and is traditionally removed after the soup course. (Food is never served on the dish itself.) The traditional reason for this added layer is that a polite table never appears in company without being properly "dressed." But I like service plates for another reason: my more-the-merrier design philosophy. Service plates can also enliven your regular good china without significant investment. Try a bright red lacquered service plate under a traditional Christmas service for a jolt of contemporary color. A "gold" lacquered plate could give your handsome-but-not-very-exciting wedding-band china a new lease on life. A tartan service plate beneath gleaming white porcelain provides a sporty look; silver plate adds elegance.

Think beyond red, green, and gold. The cobalt blue and orange pattern of Japanese Imari plates could look stunning with a blue tablecloth and rust-red napkins, surrounding a centerpiece of chrysanthemums and bittersweet. When planning your menu, consider the plates you will be serving the food on. Christmas ham might clash with the red flowers on your dinner service. *Boule de neige* could disappear on white dessert plates, but looks stunning on raspberry pink ones.

Bring out your good silver for the holidays, but don't polish it too vigorously. (Silver has become a generic name for flatware or cutlery regardless of what it is made of.) Silver looks best with a bit of patina on it. Feel free to mix antique and new pieces, different patterns, and sterling silver, silver plate, and vermeil.

Likewise, you can mix cut and mold-blown crystal and a variety of patterns. Depending on how formal your dinner is and how many wines you will be serv-

The Advent wreath is a traditional Christmas centerpiece, properly made with three white candles and one red candle. Here, Douglas fir, Colorado blue spruce, juniper, white pine, and lady apples are laced with gossamer ribbon. Wrapped party favors await guests.

ing, you'll want at least a water tumbler or goblet and one or more wineglasses. Water glasses may be made of colored glass, but wine goblets are typically clear to allow you to see the color of the wine. I have often marveled how a table can look pretty, but until the glasses are placed on it, it is somehow lacking in life. The light-catching surfaces add another dimension to the table, as well as a mood of festivity. When filled with water or wine, they become even more animated.

A one-of-a-kind centerpiece is the finishing touch for your holiday table, but that's not to say that you should think about it last. In fact, you need to plan carefully from the start so that the centerpiece will work with the table settings in terms of both scale and aesthetics. An overpowering centerpiece makes it impossible to talk to the guests seated across the table. (At a buffet table, of course, height is of no concern.) If an arrangement is tall, it must be open, like a a bouquet of orchids and curly willow. If it is lush, it should be no more than twelve inches high. If you want to go all out with a large, towering arrangement, enjoy its drama during pre-dinner drinks and hors d'oeuvres, then remove it to the sideboard just before dinner. Or, place larger centerpieces on the sideboard and serve dessert and coffee buffet-style so everyone gets a good look at them. (See "The Art of Display," page 138, for more on centerpieces.)

The Romance of Candlelight

Everyone looks younger and more attractive in candlelight; even food benefits from its forgiving light. But do make sure to have enough light so that your guests can see well. There is nothing sadder than two upright, uptight candlesticks standing alone on the table except perhaps the guests squinting to see what is on their plates. Candles come in a huge variety (see "Waxen Wonders," page 133), but whatever you choose, use them in abundance for their romantic glow and their illuminating powers. Most votive holders are made of clear, faceted, or frosted glass, but as a color freak, I love to see them in jewel-tone-cut crystal holders that suggest tiny stained-glass windows. Or place tiny tea lights in glass-lined saltcellars. Taller candles provide general illumination and should be placed above eye level so they do not distract from the faces of other diners. I do feel perfumed candles do not belong at the table, where they fight with the scent of flowers and the aroma of food.

The selection of candles is largely influenced by the candleholders you are using. If you have wonderful silver or cut-crystal candelabra, you may want to let them be the star and go with classic white or ecru candles. For playful elegance, drape them with ivy, satin ribbon, or delicate glass garlands. *Bobèches* are glass cup rings designed to sit at the base of the candle where they can catch dripping wax before it falls on the tablecloth. Some *bobèches* have holes for hanging cut crystals, enhancing their reflectivity. Brass candlesticks can look wonderful with green or red candles, assuming this works with your tablecloth and china.

When the table is set, the candles are lighted, the flowers are arranged, Bing Crosby is crooning on the stereo, and the doorbell rings, pretend that the curtain is about to rise on opening night of your new production. As you welcome your guests, succumb to the ambiance you have created. Let the play begin!

LITTLE NICETIES

Christmas comes but once a year, so why not pull out all the stops? The following little touches make the occasion even more romantic.

- Tie a tiny wreath or spray of holiday greenery to the back of each dining chair to beckon guests to the table.
- At each place setting, set out a tiny topiary Christmas tree.
- No need to pass. Set out individual salt and pepper cellars for each guest or have two guests share them.
- Place candy dishes full of bonbons or mints around the table at dessert time.
- Offer finger bowls filled with rose-scented water and rose petals before the dessert course.
- Place decanters filled with after-dinner drinks, and tied with festive ribbons, on the table after dessert.

The Naked Truth

When it comes to trees, whether to choose a natural or artificial one is the main question. Advocates of both camps make compelling arguments—the choice is up to you. Here's what you need to consider before you decide.

REAL CHOICES

A fresh-cut tree connects us to the natural world and the customs of our forefathers. In 1999, there were approximately 35.6 million fresh-cut Christmas trees sold in North America, according to the National Christmas Tree-Growers Association (NCTA). And no wonder! Many of us experience a visceral response to the resinous scent of a recently harvested tree. Buying or cutting down a living tree may be a

Before you bring the tree into the house, remove the wrapping so the branches can relax. It can stay outside in a protected area so long as it is kept in water.

family ritual. When I was a child, I used to have a recurrent nightmare that my parents would choose a Christmas tree without me. When ours finally did come home, I felt a real emotional bond with the tree. It was like a friend, a spirit guide tucked in the corner of the living room.

Cutting down a Christmas tree is not environmentally irresponsible so long as you dispose of it properly after the holidays. Christmas trees are cultivated, just like corn, soybeans, and other crops. The following spring, growers plant two or three new seedlings for each tree harvested. It can take as many as fifteen years to grow a six-foot tree (the median size when a tree is harvested), but the average growing time is seven years. The roughly one million acres devoted to growing Christmas trees provide enough oxygen each day for millions of people, according to the NCTA.

Using a living tree with its roots balled in burlap is another option, but this takes some planning. In frost-prone climates, you need to dig a hole of appropriate size before the ground freezes and you cannot keep the decorated tree in an area where the temperature rises above 60°F. Plan on keeping the tree in the house no longer than a week; otherwise it may go out of dormancy. You also must keep the burlap-covered root ball moist by setting it in a large watertight container. Even with all these precautions, adjusting from outdoor temperatures to a heated interior and then returning to the cold can deliver a fatal shock. All too many well-intentioned people see their prized blue spruce or white pine wither and die after planting. If you live in a mild climate and keep the tree in a garden room or a screen porch for just a few days, you can probably achieve success. Consider your climate and speak to someone at your nursery before deciding on a living tree.

FAVORITE SPECIES

Once you've decided on a real tree, you need to settle on a specific species. Trees should be cut after a hard freeze, when they go into dormancy and the pores in the needles close up. Needle color and shape are two important criteria, but so is needle retention. A tree that is naturally drought-resistant is better able to handle the 10 percent humidity typical inside a house without shedding. Needle length, stiffness, and sharpness also vary significantly: Some needles are soft, but others are sharp enough to live up to their name, requiring you to don gloves to trim the tree. Some species are better able to support the weight of light strings and ornaments; some have branches that allow ornaments to hang vertically; others are so shrublike that ornaments tend to rest on the branches. Finally, some kinds are more aromatic than others. There are numerous species grown in this country as Christmas trees, but the top sellers are balsam fir, Douglas fir, Fraser fir, noble fir, Scotch (or Scots) pine, Virginia pine, and white pine. Your choice of tree should suit your decorating style.

Pines tend to have longer needles than most other evergreens—some are as long as three inches—and their resin is highly aromatic. Pine needles feel relatively soft when you brush against them, and the boughs are very pliant, meaning they cannot hold too much weight. Pines tend to have good needle retention. One pine commonly used for Christmas trees is the Scotch pine, which has needles that may be dark green or bluish green. This introduced species is very hardy, making it a favorite of Christmas tree growers. White pine is particularly fluffy and very soft to the touch and has the longest needles of any Christmas tree. Virginia pine is often propagated in the southeastern United States.

Pines continue to be popular as Christmas trees because they remind people of the trees they knew when they were children. Because the boughs bend under weight, they can serve well only if you have small, light ornaments and don't use a lot of lights. And since they are typically sheared for a dense conical look, pines are well suited to decorating with ribbons and garlands wrapped around the tree. On the other hand, if a pine is not sheared, its boughs remain stronger and more able to hold heavy ornaments. If you are aiming for a minimalist approach, a pine may be an excellent choice. To my eye, however, pines are like floppy puppy dogs in habit and are better suited to the backyard, not the living room.

Spruces are another popular choice, particularly the Colorado blue spruce, thanks to its bluish-gray to silvery blue color and pungent aroma. The tree has a naturally symmetrical form, so it tends not to need as much shearing as some species. The result is a tree with growing tips that seem to reach out for ornaments. Spruces make good Christmas trees because their strong, horizontal branches can support the weight of many lights and heavy ornaments. Moreover, the trees tend to have good separation between branches, allowing ornaments to be displayed to advantage.

One disadvantage of the blue spruce is that the four-sided needles are sharply pointed, a consideration if you have young children in the house. When decorating, gloves are essential. Another problem: Spruce needles simply don't have the retentive qualities of pines and firs. This disadvantage can be overcome by cutting a blue spruce at a tree farm to ensure freshness, and by being vigilant about keeping it hydrated. Spruces are heavy drinkers, consuming up to a gallon of water overnight, and once a tree goes dry, you're done for. But handled properly, it can last six to eight weeks. The blue spruce's popularity as an ornamental means that it is often the tree of choice when selecting a living tree to plant after the holiday season. Other spruces grown as Christmas trees include the Norway spruce and white spruce, which have true green foliage.

Firs, in my opinion, make the best Christmas trees. The balsam and Fraser firs, which share many characteristics but grow in different ranges, boast dark-green or blue-green foliage respectively. Both possess an attractive open form with horizontal branches, long-lasting nee-

After you purchase your tree, the seller should wrap it in protective netting or a plastic bag. Make sure that the wrapped tree is placed on the top of your car with the tip pointing to the rear, so that the upswept branches will not be facing into the wind. Once you are home, take off the netting or plastic bag. If you are not putting the tree up right away, store it in an unheated garage, porch, or other area where it will not be subjected to wind and freezing temperatures. Within four to six hours after the tree is cut, a sap seal will form over the stump and it will stop absorbing water. (This is one reason it is so crucial to purchase your tree as early as possible.) To refresh the tree, cut one inch off the base of the trunk and place it in a bucket of warm water. Water is the single most important way to keep your tree fresh for the duration of the season. According to NCTA, there is no need to add sugar, bleach, or any commercial preparation; in fact, they could do damage. Even if you plan to bring the tree into the house right away, allow twenty-four hours for the branches to relax after being compressed in the netting. You can keep a tree outside for several weeks, as long as it is kept in a protected area and its drinking water is never allowed to evaporate.

After you bring the tree indoors, make another cut a quarter to half an inch from the base. Cut at a neat right angle to the tree trunk to ensure stability; there is no absorption advantage to a diagonal cut. Then place the tree in a sturdy stand that holds at least a gallon of water. Again, continue to replenish the liquid to ensure that the tree does not dry out. If you purchased your tree at a cutting farm, it will not absorb as much water as an already cut tree, which will be thirstier.

If by chance you forgot to make a fresh cut before decorating the tree, you will have to remove the decorations, make the cut, and redecorate. Alternatively, drill half-inch holes in the base of the trunk half an inch apart, which might allow the tree to again absorb water. Then be sure to keep the water level above the holes.

dles about an inch long, and enduring balsam fragrance. The Canaan fir is similar to the balsam and Fraser firs, and has dark green needles with a silvery underside. The Douglas fir, although it hails from a different horticultural family than true firs, has long been grown as a Christmas tree and it is a traditional favorite for good reason. The spreading, often drooping branches are well spaced, allowing excellent ornament display, and the boughs are dense enough to hide many strings of lights. The short needles are soft to the touch and radiate out in all directions from the branch, giving a lush appearance. The needles on the grand fir, in contrast, are set in two distinct rows and are usually horizontally spread so that both the upper and lower sides of the branches are clearly visible. The Lincoln Douglas fir, a variety native to the high desert of New Mexico, has the ability to survive in a dry climate, giving it exceptional longevity as a cut tree. The white fir, also known as concolor fir, has good foliage color and a pleasing natural shape and aroma; the flat, narrow needles measure between two and three inches in length, and have good holding power. My personal favorite is the noble fir, grown in the Pacific Northwest but increasingly available nationwide, which has a beautiful shape, stiff branches, and an ability to

CLOCKWISE FROM TOP LEFT: **Common Christmas tree species include balsam fir, Scotch pine, Douglas fir, Fraser fir, and Colorado blue spruce.**

stay fresh for a long time.

I order my fresh trees from Eric and Gloria Sundback, who run a tree farm in West Virginia and have been named the National Champion Grower by the National Christmas Tree-Growers Association three times. The National Champion is awarded the privilege of supplying the 18-foot tree for the Blue Room in the White House. Each tree the Sundbacks sell is a work of art. After experimenting with many tree species, they have settled on Douglas and Fraser firs. The couple advocates a style of pruning that differs from the annual shearing that most growers use to shape their trees as they ready them for market. The result is a tree with branches that reach out like fingers and enough openness between branches to display ornaments to advantage. According to Eric Sundback, to encourage branches strong enough to support heavy ornaments, you have to thin some branches to promote the growth of others. And, he explains, "Like a desk with pigeonholes to store items, you want the spaces between branches to be uniform."

Starting in a tree's third year, most growers use a hay mover set on its side to shear trees. When the tip of a branch is cut off by this method, its natural response is to form two new tips, creating a denser, bushier, shrublike habit. In contrast to this buzz-cut treatment, the Sundbacks shingle their trees by removing an entire branch, and never cutting mid-branch, aiming for a separation between branches of about twelve inches. I wish more Christmas tree growers would adopt the Sundbacks' methods. Although it takes more time to prune by hand than by machine, it produces more beautiful, natural-looking trees that are worth paying a little extra for.

In the wild, blue spruces, shown here, and other species rarely achieve the perfect shape of trees cultivated on Christmas tree farms, but their majesty is undeniable.

THE ART OF ARTIFICE

Artificial trees may seem less charming than the real McCoy, but they are neater—no needles to vacuum up; they are safer—most are fire-resistant, and they are easier to put up and take down.

Some even come with lights permanently attached, and many can be stored for the following year with light strings attached, representing a significant savings in time. A quality artificial tree can look incredibly real and display perfect form if properly fluffed up. When covered with ornaments, a top-of-the-line model will fool most casual observers.

Artificial trees were first manufactured in Germany in the 1880s after the passion for real *Tannenbäume* had led to serious deforestation. Replicas were made with goose or turkey feathers wrapped around wood and wire frames. Most were designed for tabletop use. In the United States, brush trees (the same machinery made toilet brushes!) were capable of handling heavier decorations.

Artificial trees now come in all sizes and with a range of features. Most are made of vinyl. A top-of-the-line eight-foot tree might run $450 to $500, whereas a bargain-basement model might cost less than $100. A tree should not only look convincingly realistic, it also must be strong enough to bear the weight of thousands of lights and hundreds of ornaments. One significant advantage of a quality artificial tree over a real one is that it can withstand a greater load.

Christopher Krupa, a designer with The Curio Cabinet and Christmas Village of Olde Worthington, a Radko Starlight store in Worthington, Ohio, who has been buying and selling artificial trees for a dozen years, offers the following advice:

Determine the size first. Measure the height of the room in which you will place the tree. I like to see about a foot between the top of the tree topper and the ceiling, so take that space into consideration when ascertaining height.

- Artificial trees come in a variety of shapes from very narrow ones called "pencils" to others with a width more than half their height. When deciding on diameter, allow for some breathing space so the tree is not jammed up against a wall or a piece of furniture. Width should not be confused with fullness. The more branches, the more tips on each branch, and the more needles on each tip, the lusher the tree. Also, some trees brush the floor; others sit several inches off of it.

- The look of the tree is also determined by needle length and color. Traditional looks mimic Fraser fir, blue spruce, white pine, and other species. Naturalistic colors range from green to blue-green, or blue-green mixed with green. Flocked trees imitate the look of snow on branches. More fantastical looks include white, silver, gold, even burgundy red and hot pink! Tinsel trees come in a variety of metallic hues . A fiber-optic tree made of light-refracting plastic filaments is an otherworldly option. These trees rotate slowly, allowing colors to burst forth from every branch.

- The final factor is to determine which of three construction methods you prefer. Most artificial trees' branches have hooks that slide into rings on the center pole and can be removed for storage. A hinged tree has branches that fold up for storage, rather like an umbrella. Look for metal, not plastic, hinges for durability. A significant benefit of the hinged design is that you can store it with lights intact. (The hook-on branch design can also be stored with its lights, but only if you use one string of lights on each branch; you have to connect each string after you put the tree back together.) A third style, the panel tree, separates into two or three segments. Branches hook onto a ring at the top and rest on a metal circle like a hoop skirt.

To ascertain quality, check that the center pole is made of metal, wood, or a tree trunk—not plastic. Branches should be attached to the pole with at least three and preferably four rivets, screws, or anchors. The tree should come with a stand. A really good tree will have a ten-year warranty.

Prelit trees can be a tremendous timesaver, but you have to make sure both the tree and the lights are of comparable quality. Also, although a prelit tree comes with extra bulbs, if a whole section has to be replaced, it could be hard to match the lights exactly. Finally, you may not be able to find a tree that is as heavily lit as you like.

Before stringing an artificial tree with lights, it is essential that it be shaped, meaning the branches fluffed up and needles straightened out, to maximize its beauty and verisimilitude. At the ends of the branches, the longest tip should be horizontal and curved slightly up as though it is reaching for the light. The object is to mimic the look of a living tree.

Index